Stop Wishing and Start Living

Barb Frye
with Greg Smith

Black Lake Press
TELL YOUR STORY
BLACKLAKEPRESS.COM

Black Lake Press
TELL YOUR STORY
BLACKLAKEPRESS.COM

Cover design by Greg Smith of Black Lake Studio.

Published by Black Lake Press of Holland, Michigan.
Black Lake Press is a division of Black Lake Studio, LLC.
Direct inquiries to Black Lake Press at
www.blacklakepress.com.

ISBN 978-0-9883373-1-2

Dedication

I dedicate this book to my parents, Nancy and Jay. I would not be the person I am today without their unconditional love and support. Mom, I will always be grateful for your patient and understanding heart, from which I have drawn so much of my strength. Dad, I thank God for you and miss you everyday. Thank you for teaching me how to become the person I want to be.

To my son Max: you bring the greatest love and happiness to my life. You are my whole world and the reason I go on everyday. I could not imagine my life without you!

Table of Contents

Acknowledgements

To my sister Kim and late brother Dave, I love you both. To my husband Don, thank you for believing in me and supporting me day after day.

To my friends, new and old, near and far... your energy and encouragement has kept me going all these years. Thank you for supporting me and my family through all the ups and downs.

Thank you to Katy Major ('Katy's') for your hours of reading and editing my chapters and correcting my horrific English... love you, Katy's!

Nancy Wilson, whom I went to early in this endeavor and who was the first to start the editing process, thank you for your encouragement to keep me writing.

Thank you to Lisa Hostler for all your editing and suggestions.

Ann Moran and Katie Payne-Confer, thank you for believing my story would make a difference in a person's life. You both planted the seed in my mind to put my story on paper, and I love you both for your support!

And to Linda and Bud Myers, you were there at the hospital early that Sunday morning for my parents and have always been there for my family throughout the years. I love you both always!

Foreword

I first met Barb at a Students Against Drunk Driving workshop in 1987. I was the host at this event but Barb was the star. High school kids from all over Northeastern Ohio were glued in their seats as she told her story from her wheel chair. She told them that just a few years before this date, she'd been just like them. Funny thing is though, Barb isn't like anyone I've ever met before. I have had the opportunity to work with her a few more times since that event and she has always made everyone she comes in contact with feel better about life .

Fast forward to 2002... As I was leaving a store I watched in great humility as a woman, alone, got her four-year-old son into a van and strapped him into his car seat. She then positioned her wheel chair into the driver's seat area and started off. It broke my heart and made me incredibly proud of this woman all at the same time. Through my tears, I realized it was Barb.

Since reconnecting with Barb, I have been honored to share her story with my television viewers. However, it's the friendship we share that is most special to me. She's beautiful. She's deep. She's funny. She loves life and all the crazy, zany things life throws her way. Her zest for life and amazing attitude about it is reflected throughout her story. As you read this book, I hope you find Barb's story motivating and inspiring. Barb's message is about a choice that we all have—a choice to stop wishing and start living the life we have today!

—Robin Swoboda, *Channel 3 News, Cleveland, Ohio*

Preface

The Accident

I remember lying there, motionless, in a crumpled ball on the ceiling of the car. It was dark all around me. I could hear someone screaming my name and crying. I wanted to yell out to them, but there was no sound coming from my mouth. I was trying to breathe. Trying to get air in my lungs to yell, but–nothing. I felt like I was suffocating. Every breath seemed like my last. What was wrong with me? Why couldn't I breathe?

I lay there for what seemed like eternity, hoping that this was just a dream. I lay there thinking to myself that if I closed my eyes and opened them back up again, everything would be fine. *Dear God, please let this be just a bad dream.*

I opened my eyes and nothing was different. I tried to keep myself calm so that I could keep breathing, but my mind was racing. Racing to put together what happen. I remembered seeing headlights and my friend cutting the wheel as hard as she could to avoid hitting the lights that were coming at us. It all happened so quickly. The flipping. The impact into the ditch. And then everything stopped. Why couldn't I move anything?

Is this what it's like to die? I'm only eighteen years old. I'm not supposed to die yet. Life was not supposed to happen like this. This was not supposed to happen to me. I was simply going on a car ride with my friend, and then I would go home, like all the other car rides before. But this one was different. I was not going home. Not for a very long time.

That night, I learned that our lives can change in an instant. Since that night, I've learned that those instants don't have to change us. That's what this book is about: what can change in our lives and what doesn't have to.

Do I wish that I hadn't made the choices that led me to be upside down in that car? Sure, but I did make them. They are a part of my life story, which I'm going to try and tell you in these pages. It's the only life I will ever have. I could have changed my behavior before the accident, but there are no do-overs. There's no point in wishing I had a different story to tell you. This is the only life I will ever have.

Obviously, I didn't die that night. Many things in my life changed, which I will tell you about in the chapters ahead. But some things didn't. I didn't stop being me. My family didn't stop loving me. I could still fall in love. I could still learn and laugh, and my future was still my responsibility, to become whoever I chose to be. Yes, my career options were more limited—I couldn't be a prima ballerina, for example–but that wasn't going to happen anyway, accident or no accident. But my character continued to be mine to choose.

Since that night my life has gone down a different road than it would have if the accident hadn't happened. But I have no idea what the other road, or roads, would have held in store for me. The only path I've ever known, or could have ever known, is the one that I've actually taken. Everything else is just imagination.

So I kept on living my only life, making the best of it. I hope that as you read my story, you will think about which parts of your own life you can control and which ones you can't. You can choose your actions, but you can't make choices for other people. You can minimize risks in life, but you can't eliminate them. You can't make every day fun, but you can find what's funny in each situation and laugh out loud about it. You can take life seriously but learn to not take yourself too seriously. You can be sorry when you've done something wrong, but you don't have to feel sorry for yourself. You can get hurt, but you don't have to hurt others.

Right now, today, you can choose to be smarter and live more safely. Right now, today, you can decide to be resilient and determined to be as happy as you can be. Right now, today, you can rejoice over even small blessings and reject negative thoughts and nasty behaviors. You can make the effort to learn something today and to share it with someone. You can say please and thank you and I love you to the people around you. You can do all these things because even if you end up upside down in a car, you won't stop being you. I know this for certain, because I did, and I didn't.

You can choose to not do something you might regret later, but what about those things that you already did that you regret now? The things that are in your cracked rear view mirror? Here's what I discovered: they are a permanent part of your story. They can't and won't go away. We all get dealt some bad cards, and sometimes we play good cards poorly. But once the hand is played, it's done. It's time to move on, learn from your mistakes, and play the next hand better.

Yes, in an instant the circumstances of your life can change forever. But people don't change in an instant, or they don't have to. Who we are, our essential character, has more momentum than that. You may not be able to choose your parents, your physical health, where you live, or what happens to those you love, but you can choose who you will be in the midst of it all.

That night in the car, I began to learn the most important lesson of my life: that I can choose life. This life. And if I have any advice to give, it comes down to this: live the hell out of the life you've got, love the people around you (and love a few of them intensely), and laugh a lot.

Chapter One

Growing Up

Growing up, I was a very active kid. I was the youngest of three children born to Jay and Nancy Eisenhart. My mom said that if I were her firstborn, I would have been an only child. That statement alone reveals what kind of baby I was. My sister, Kim, is five years older than me, and my brother David falls between us.

I was born in Akron in April, 1966. My family lived in Munroe Falls, a suburb of Akron, for the first two years of my life and then moved us out to the country. I was brought up in Medina County, and I have resided there ever since.

My father worked in the insurance industry and my mom was a registered nurse. As a convenience of my parent's professions, my siblings and I could get hurt and mom would fix it. If she couldn't fix it, we at least had my dad's insurance. But there was a definite downside to having a nurse for a mom. No dirt bikes or you'll break your legs. No trampolines or you'll break your neck. And certainly no BB guns, because if you do, you will shoot your eye out. Basically, as a kid, life was no fun.

David and Kim were closer in age, eighteen months apart; therefore, they formed a close friendship. I was the tag-a-long little sister that they always had to include in their activities. I'm sure, at any point growing up, that they would have loved it if I had gotten lost somewhere and if my parents never searched for me. But I was their sister, and it didn't look like my parents planned on losing me anytime soon. So they had no choice but to put up with me.

Today my sister and I are very close. When she went off to Ohio State for college, that was the turning point in our sibling relationship. We no longer had to share a bedroom, and we became friends again. I would be lost without her now.

We were a middle-class family. Both my parents worked and made sure that we had everything. Not everything in the way of material stuff, but everything as far as family support and care went. My parents never missed one of our sporting events, and they always made sure we went on awesome family vacations. These were the important things my parents knew we needed in life.

I remember my mom would work the night shift at the hospital so she didn't miss any of our daytime events. She would come home after working all night, sleep a couple of hours, and then get up to take us where we needed to go.

Whether it was to a sport practice or a friend's house, my mom made sure we got to our destinations. Regardless of if she was running on only three and a half hours of sleep and had to work again that night, my mom did it. That's why she was and still is "The World's Greatest Mom."

My parents were pretty strict as well. They always knew who our friends were growing up and usually were very good friends with their parents. My sister and brother had curfews when they would go out, and God help them if they where late. My parents had an expectation of how we should act when we were out. If we didn't behave well, we'd be in for it. We were expected to know right from wrong. My dad would say, "Just use common sense, damn it!" He was not a yeller, but he certainly had a way with words. My dad also had this look to him that made us wish we were somewhere else.

My mom, on the other hand, could yell. Of course, she couldn't understand why *she* had to yell and my father didn't. But she did it anyway. I remember clearly how she yelled when my brother was on the field during a football game. I can hear her now, "God damn it David, tackle!" Her voice carried over everyone else's cheers and heckles, and it even cut through the noise of the band. When I would hear her bellow this out, it reassured me that my parents were still at the game. Not that I thought they would have left me, but it definitely was comforting to know my parents were always there.

As is typical in parental language, I was not without a catchy adjective that was often used before my name. I remember when I was doing something I shouldn't have been doing, or simply because she had 'had it' with me, I was lovingly addressed as "Jesus Christ Barbara." So if I heard, "Jesus Christ Barbara, God damn it," I knew David was in trouble, too. By hearing this often, it became second nature to us to know that both David and I were in for it.

So basically, mom could get her point across to us kids quite vocally. For some reason, though, Kim didn't get a catchy adjective before her name. Of course, this must have been because she was my parents' favorite (laugh out loud). This favorite kid game seems to run its course in every family.

But, as I look back on those restrictions now, my mom and dad had good reason to not let us kids *do* some of those things or *have* some of those things. Seeing the worst while working in the Emergency Room caused my mom to fear the worst. We had restrictions and boundaries, and we knew we would have consequences if we abused them. I would later test out these restrictions when I got into high school.

When my family first moved to Medina, we lived in a quaint farmhouse that was next to a huge horse-boarding farm. The farm had forty or more stalls and a large indoor riding arena. My sister, brother, and I spent most of our adolescent years hanging out at the barn.

The summer days were spent bailing hay and hanging out with the other kids around the barn. We would spend hours in the hayloft building forts out of the hay, and when it got dark, we would play hide-and-go-seek. Spending so much of our time playing at the barn allowed us to get to know the owners well. Eventually, we even gave them the affectionate title of "Uncle" before their actual names.

For Kim, Dave, and I, it was a great way to grow up with never ending adventures. Most of our friends would want to come over to play at our house. My parents liked this, too, because that way they would know where we were and who we were with.

One of my best friends growing up was a girl named Jennifer Thompson. Jennifer and I were inseparable. Jen, as almost everyone called her, lived in a development where we could walk to the neighbors' houses and ride our bikes up and down the street. Jen loved to come to my house and play in the fields and ride horses. I, on the other hand, wanted to go to Jennifer's house and ride bikes on the street and watch MTV. Jennifer's family had cable TV —the *good* television.

Jen and I would spend as much time as we could together. We attended the same elementary school, and if Jen was not getting off the bus at my house for the weekend, I was getting off the bus at hers. When Jen was at my house, we loved going next door to the barn to play. We would take the two ponies that belonged to the owners and go riding back in the fields. We would ride through the woods, pretending we were running from bad guys. Don't ask me who the bad guys were; we would just make up adventures and act them out as the day went on.

There is one story I remember vividly and still laugh at today. Jen and I had been riding in the woods and fields all day, and it was time to head back to the barn. It was close to dinnertime, not only for Jen and I, but also for Charlie and Dutch Boy, the ponies we were on. If anyone has horses or ponies, you know that animals know when it is feeding time.

Knowing that it was time to head back, we started to canter our ponies. Instead of a nice ride back to the barn, they took off in a full gallop. Jen and I were holding on to the reins and horns of the saddles for dear life. With our hair whipping through the wind, it was full throttle back to the barn.

Dutch Boy, the little black pony that Jen rode, had a habit of stopping. Without any warning, he would go from a full gallop to an abrupt stop, lowering his head to the ground to nibble on some grass. Well, I forgot to tell Jen about this little habit of Dutch Boy's. As I was galloping along on Charlie, I could see Jen in my peripheral vision galloping along next to me. Then, sure enough, as we made our way over the hill on the home stretch back to the barn, Jen was no longer in my line of sight. I slowed my pony down and looked back. I could see Dutch Boy eating away at the grass but no Jen. My eyes scanned the field for my friend, and there she was, lying face-down in the grass. Thank God, she was not hurt. Although it was a scary moment, we still look back on that ride today and laugh. This was just one of our adventures over at the barn.

In 1977, we moved away from the barn and into the house my parents still own today. We were still in Medina County, but we were now closer to the junior high and high school that my sister, brother, and I were attending. Since we all were involved in so many school activities, mom and dad figured it would be more practical to live closer. It was sad leaving that old farmhouse and all the memories, but there were more memories to be made.

Chapter Two

High School Years

I was in junior high when one of my teachers told my mom at a parent-teacher conference that I was a "femme fatal," a woman who attracts men by an aura of charm. (Don't worry, I had to look it up too.) As it turns out, the teacher hit the nail right on the head.

At the ripe age of thirteen, I discovered boys, and the boy craze began. Along with this discovery, I learned the art of flirting. I don't think I really had to work very hard at the flirting thing too much–it just came naturally. I wish I could say that I had the same natural knack for mathematics, but I guess we can't have everything.

Besides being introduced to boys in junior high, I was also introduced to cheerleading. And once I became acquainted with cheerleading, I knew I had found my passion. Nothing made me happier than being in front of people, cheering, and performing. Although my desire to play other sports like softball and volley ball continued, cheerleading was my favorite.

School was more or less just a social event for me. I had okay grades, but I usually only applied myself enough to get by. Sure, I appreciated learning and being taught, but I was mostly going to school to be with my friends and to have fun.

My social network in junior high and high school was mainly the jocks and the popular kids. My friends and I would hang out at one of our houses, where we would watch TV or listen to music. Video game systems were limited to Atari back then, and if you had one, you were considered rich. (Needless to say, my family did not have one.) So, my friends and I watched MTV a lot (this was when MTV actually showed music videos) and just basically hung out. As long as we were together, we didn't really care what we did.

When I look at how simple life was back then compared to now, I feel thankful that I grew up when I did. We didn't have cell phones. There was no Facebook or Twitter. Or is it Tweeter? Do I tweet on the Twitter or twit on the Tweeter? I always get so confused by this... Anyway, there was none of this social networking stuff when I grew up. If we wanted to make a call to a friend, we used the kitchen house phone and sat on the counter to talk to them. Believe it or not, we actually had a phone mounted on the wall, not stuck in our jeans pocket! There was no privacy or going off to our rooms to talk alone. The most privacy my siblings and I ever got was when we managed to stretch the phone cord around the corner of the kitchen wall far enough to reach the basement steps. We would sit on the steps and talk for hours in private.

Over time, though, the phone cord started to wear out from being stretched, and wires started showing where the cord went into the hand receiver. My father said, "Once that cord goes, there will be no other cord!" So when my father put that disclaimer out there, we treasured that phone cord. It was our lifeline out!

In high school, I would talk on the phone to my friends for hours. I would call my girlfriends all the time. Calling boys, however, was another story. My mother believed that a young woman should not call a boy. She believed it was proper for a boy to call a girl instead. Hello, nineteen forties! Of course, if they were just friends, I could call. So we'll just say I had a lot of boys that were *just* friends.

One other thing we had to be aware of while using the phone was long distance calling. See, there were no "in-network" or "friends-and-family" phone plans back then. It was either a local call or a long distance call, plain and simple. And of course, it seemed like all my friends were long distance. So, at the beginning of every month when the phone bill came, I had to hear the wrath of my father.

My father had a favorite saying when describing me to someone; he used to say, "I think she was born with a phone in her hand." I could count on it every time someone asked my dad about me. It was a humorous consolation to my mother, who, to this day, believes I was born with the "gift of gab."

This reminds me of a funny story. When my niece stayed with my family for a few weeks while she was in high school, she and I had a conversation one evening about her going out with some of her friends. At that time, she was a senior in high school, and if I remember correctly, she was eighteen years old. I can't remember hearing where she said she was going, but I told her to be home by midnight. I distinctly remember my father's words echoing in my head as I said to her, "If you're out past midnight, you are getting into trouble."

My niece's response to me was, "Well, if I'm late, I'll call you." This makes me laugh because when I was her age, we were not late—period. We made *sure* not to be late. So I informed her that it would not be necessary for her to call me because she was *not* going to be late.

If I close my eyes I can still see the look on her face. Her face said it all so innocently. "What? What do you mean?" Kids never seem to remember that the adults in their lives were once teenagers too. It was almost like she had already planned on being late and that it was okay if she was. She would just call.

I informed her that at her age, I was not allowed to be late, and neither was she. Of course, I got the eye roll and that typical teenager "whatever look," which was okay–I understood that look all too well. That night after our talk, she came home safe and sound. And, if I remember correctly, she even came home fifteen minutes early.

With technology today and all the resources that kids have available to them at the touch of their fingers, rules and responsibilities seem very flexible and open to negotiation and suggestion. If only my girlfriends and I had cell phones! We would have been able to just call our parents and tell them we were at the mall and that we would be late getting home, when really, we would have been at a boy's house in the next town over doing God knows what.

I do believe there does need to be a certain amount of trust between a parent and their kids. And, at some point, a parent needs to believe they raised their children to know right from wrong. My parents, for the most part, did trust us and did teach us well. But with technology comes freedom, with freedom comes curiosity, and with curiosity comes the choice to experiment.

The Internet alone is like having the world on a screen, right in front of us. And with one click or a scroll we can find *everything*. The more I think about this, the more I think I was better off without today's modern conveniences. All the technological gadgets of today would have ended up being another thing to experiment with. And knowing myself and knowing most of my friends well, we would have certainly used them to get in trouble. Heck,

I probably would have invented "sexting." Okay, maybe I'm exaggerating my "badness" a bit, but believe me, I had no problem getting into trouble–the old fashion way.

Speaking of trouble and experimenting, I was in junior high when I first tried alcohol. What drew me to using it at such a young age? I tried it mainly out of simple curiosity. I had seen my parents drink alcohol before, so to me, it probably didn't seem that bad to try it. According to a statistic on teenhelp.com, fifty-one percent of eighth graders have tried alcohol, and roughly half that amount admits to drinking to get drunk. This study supports my belief that the earlier one experiments with alcohol, the more likely one is to use and abuse alcohol.

Throughout my high school years, my alcohol use increased. After football games, basketball games, or really any other school activity, my friends and I would get together and party. For the most part, the parties involved alcohol. Usually we didn't need a reason to drink. If we won a game, lost a game, or tied a game, we would party and drink.

There seemed to be a party every weekend during my years of high school. I would go to the parties with the same group of girlfriends that I always hung out with. We would drink and have fun and just celebrate for any reason.

Some parties were better than others. By better I mean there was more alcohol and very limited parental control.

Also, if there was not a good party going on within our school district, my girlfriends and I would hear about a party in a nearby district and go to that.

Sometimes my friends and I would pre-drink before a party. If one of my friends' parents was not home, we would pre-drink at their house. However, the majority of the pre-drinking occurred in the car.

As far as picking a designated driver for safety, the "DD" was usually the person who drank the least. Which, of course, is *not* the correct definition. But we figured that by doing this we were being semi-responsible.

My friends and I didn't really worry about the dangers of drinking and driving. What we worried about was getting caught by the cops. If I would have been pulled over for drinking and driving and charged with a DWI, DUI, or OVI, the ramifications from my dad would have been *huge*! (Personally, I think that there should be an additional driving acronym: DAD—for Dumb Ass Driving!)

Yes, I remember being told, either by the instructor in driver's education class or by a police officer at our junior/senior pre-prom assembly, about the facts of drinking and driving. The authoritative figure would tell us in a stern, harsh voice that people can and do get killed. But honestly, my friends and I probably listened at that particular moment, got squeamish when the police officer told us the gory details of car accidents he had come upon, but soon forgot about the truth of those details.

Truthfully, we just figured it was never going to happen to one of us. Of course, I cannot speak for my friends, but I am sure I felt that I would beat the odds–*that* would never happen to me. Besides, we were good kids just having fun.

When I look back on why I chose to experiment with alcohol at a young age, I ask myself what factors influenced the decision I made. Several things come to mind. First, I'm sure seeing my parents drink at social events played a part in my decision. I am not saying that my parents were big drinkers, but what a parent does or how a parent acts *does* influence a child's behavior. Remember, the educational tools on alcohol use and teenagers that are provided today to parents were not as available when my siblings and I were young. My parents went by the "do as I say, not as I do" philosophy.

Another factor contributing to my early use was the fact that my older brother was a senior in high school when I was a freshman. In the late seventies and early eighties, drinking alcohol was as common as going swimming on a hot summer day. There was even a "drinking club" at my high school created by the most popular senior guys. So the lure of impressing the older guys had an effect on me.

Looking back now, I really did not like how alcohol tasted nor how it made me feel after I drank too much of it. However, that did not stop me from using it. One thing I did like about it was that it made me feel more friendly and outgoing. Ultimately, it made me feel invincible.

My friends and I would do some of the dumbest and most unsafe things ever after we had been drinking. It wasn't like we didn't know better, but the alcohol impaired our judgment. One thing I specifically remember doing was a Chinese Fire Drill. My girlfriends and I would drive around and drink. When we would come up to an intersection or red light, whoever was driving would stop, of course. The rest of us in the car would quickly jump out and run around the car several times. When the light turned green, we would quickly jump back into the car, screaming and laughing, and then we would drive off.

Of course, the fun, exciting part was when someone didn't quite make it all the way back into the car when the light turned green. Another dumb thing my friends and I would do is to jump on the hood of a friend's car as they were driving off from a party or just driving away. Were we impaired during these stunts? Most often, yes. Did my friends and I think something bad could happen to anyone of us? Most often, no. Why? Impairment is not instant. Being mentally impaired by alcohol is gradual. Impairment leads a good person to do the wrong things. Bottom line: It can radically change a person's good judgment.

Chapter Three

In an Instant

Everything was dark. I could hear my friend screaming, telling me we needed to get out of the car. But when I tried to move, I couldn't feel anything. I remember thinking, *Where are my arms? Where are my legs? Why is it so hard to breathe?* I tried everything I could to move. I tried to move my hands. *Where are my hands?* I couldn't feel them.

My head felt like it was wedged underneath something. I remember feeling an immense pressure on my head. I was later told that the pressure I was feeling was the weight of my body on top of my head. My neck had been broken, and my head had somehow been tucked up under my torso. I was crumpled in a ball on the inside of the roof of the car. The car had flipped over into a ditch and was now resting upside down. I had an overwhelming feeling of wonderment and disbelief. *What had just happened?*

This car ride was not supposed to end like this. I was supposed to get in the car, enjoy the ride, and then go back home safe and sound. I never in a million years thought that this would or could happen to me. I was in complete denial about the reality of my situation. We were not supposed to crash. Something like this doesn't happen to a person like me.

I lay in the car for probably twenty minutes before help arrived, and for those twenty minutes, which seemed like an eternity, every thought went through my mind. *My God, I'm only eighteen years old, and I'm going to die. This is not supposed to happen to me.* I thought of my parents, my brother, and my sister. When I left my sister's house earlier that night, I never told my parents that I loved them, nor did I kiss them good-bye. *Am I ever going to see them again?*

I kept trying to breathe. The longer I lay there, the harder it was to get air in my lungs. I felt like I was suffocating. I kept saying to myself over and over again, *Please God, I do not want to die.* As a college student, I was just starting my life. *My God, I'm dying.*

I remember hoping that if I just closed my eyes and opened them back up again, everything would be okay. My arms would work. My legs would work. I would be able to feel my extremities attached to my body. I closed my eyes tightly and prayed that this was all just a bad dream, but when I finally dared to open them, the world around me was still dark. I still could not move or feel anything.

I just laid there. I could hear my friend screaming and crying, and by the muffled sound of her voice, I could tell she had gotten out of the car. I tried to move, to get out, but my body wasn't responding to what my brain was telling it to do. As waves of hopelessness passed through my body, I closed my eyes again.

Hearing other voices, I opened up my eyes, and I could see flashing lights. I knew help was there. A few moments after I saw the flashing lights, I heard a gentleman's voice; he was talking to me, trying to get me to respond. I remember telling him in a faint whisper that I could not feel my arms or legs. I also asked him why there was so much pressure on my head. The gentleman, who I later found out was a police officer, knew right away that I had a serious neck injury. He knew the emergency responders would have to take every precaution getting me out of the car. He assured me that everything would be okay.

Within minutes, the rescue workers had put a large brace on my neck to completely immobilize my neck and head. They carefully untangled my body from the inside roof of the car and put me on a backboard. Two large foam blocks were placed on each side of my head, and they secured my head to the board with tape. They lifted me out of the car and loaded me into the waiting ambulance.

I think I was going in and out of shock during the time I was being pulled from the car, because I only remember bits and pieces of what was happening. I do not remember much of the ambulance ride to the hospital. I do, however, remember the ambulance workers asking me my name and phone number. I didn't have any identification on me because I had left my purse and wallet in my car. So, at the accident scene, I had no identification on me. Luckily, I was conscious, so I could give them my parents' names and phone number.

While in the ambulance, I had not yet understood the seriousness of my injuries. I remember thinking that once they got me to the hospital where the doctors could fix my injuries, I would be okay. My arms and legs would start to move, and I would be able to feel them as a part of my body again.

I was taken to Parma General Hospital where I was put in the Trauma Unit of the Emergency Room. A team of doctors and nurses began to work on me right away. My clothes were cut off of me so they could see if there were any other injuries to my body (I have been told that this is standard procedure). IVs were started, giving me fluids and medication to relax me. X-rays were ordered for my neck so the doctors could see what was going on.

If I started to get sick and wanted to throw up, there was no way they could roll me over or sit me up because of my neck. A tube was inserted through my nose to remove the contents (food and beer) of my stomach. This was not a pleasant experience.

While all this was happening to me in the hospital, my parents were getting one of the worst phone calls imaginable for a parent. A person from the ER is always assigned to make these types of phone calls, letting family know that their loved ones have been brought into the ER for some reason or another. That night, my parents were notified that their daughter had been involved in a motor vehicle accident and that they needed to get there.

Later on, I asked my mom what had been going through her head when the phone rang at 3:15 in the morning. She said that as soon as she heard the first ring, she sat straight up in bed and thought, *My God, Barbara's not home.* Since the phone was on my dad's side of the bed, he answered the early-morning phone call from Parma Hospital. Before my dad hung up the phone, my mom was already up, half dressed, and yelling at my dad to hurry up. She was asking my dad questions about who was on the phone and what they had said. My dad Jay, who is an extremely laid back man, was calm and collected and simply told my mom that it was Parma Hospital and that I had been in a car accident. My mom, on the other hand, feared the worst.

My mom, Nancy, or Fancy as I like to call her now (long story), was all emotion when it came to us kids. As I said earlier, it was my mom who was the one that we heard yelling from the stands during our sporting events. I cannot imagine what my mom was thinking at that time of the call.

My dad thought that I had probably just gone off the road while driving home from the party and I was taken to the hospital to get checked out as a precautionary measure. I don't think my dad thought it was going to be serious. My mom, on the other hand, had a bad feeling. Call it either mother's intuition or being a nurse in the Emergency Room for years and seeing the worst things ever—whatever you want to call it, my mom had a feeling that something had gone very wrong.

It was about a thirty-minute drive from my parents' house to Parma Hospital. I later would ask my mom what was going through her mind during that ride. She said that she just kept hoping I was alive and that my face and brain were okay. Whatever else was wrong with me, she would handle it.

When my parents pulled into the hospital parking lot, my dad pulled around to the ER entrance, and before my dad stopped the car, my mom was getting out. As she made her way through the ER doorway, a nurse was waiting for her in the lobby. Upon seeing the nurse, my mom knew right away that this was not a minor injury.

As I said, my mom was a nurse for years in the Emergency Room at Medina General Hospital. She had seen young kids brought into the ER with horrible injuries from car accidents or motorcycle crashes with no helmets.

Hence the reason we were never able to have a mini bike growing up. But she also remembered being a nurse having to wait at the entrance of the ER to catch the parents of these young kids and directing them to a private room. This was where the doctor would tell the parents that their child was either dead or very seriously injured. My mom would come home from working in the Emergency Room, and if there was a young person that had died, we heard about it. We would hear that she does not ever want to be in the position of the parent coming into the ER who is stopped by a nurse and lead off to that private room. So of course, we did everything we could as children to reassure her that we would never put her in that position.

My mom was now that parent being faced with dreaded news as she was stopped by a nurse. She knew that this was not good.

As the nurse said my mom's name, my mom blurted out, "She's dead isn't she?" The nurse began to answer her when my mom then said emphatically, "I'm a nurse, so do not lie to me." My dad, at this point, had joined her in the ER, and the nurse assured them both that I was alive and that the doctor would talk to them. The nurse then led my parents to "the room," where they waited for the doctor to come in.

Within minutes Dr. Larry Stern, a neurosurgeon who was on call for the Emergency Room that night, introduced himself to my parents and began to explain my condition. I had broken and dislocated my neck at my cervical 4th and 5th vertebrae and was paralyzed from the shoulders down. My parents sat there and listened as Dr. Stern explained in medical detail how he planned to treat my injury. He went on and told them that he would put me in traction and try to straighten my neck that way. I would be placed in a bed called a Circle Bed, were I would remain for the next eight weeks.

After hearing everything from Dr. Stern, the only thing my mom wanted to do was see *me*. She wanted to see that my face was not disfigured and that I was conscious. My mom knew that if my face was intact and that I had suffered no brain injury, she would ask God for strength to help me accept what had happened to me. This is very typical of my mom; she always put everyone's needs in front of her own.

I was lying on the bed in the Trauma Unit when my parents were brought in to see me. My head was still immobilized by the neck brace, so the only place I could see or look was up. As my parents made their way to the bed, one of the nurses who had been working on me stopped them and told them to only touch me on my head and shoulders. These were the only areas on my body that I could feel.

I remember my mom coming up on the right side of the bed and my dad coming up on my left. I started crying and telling them that I was so sorry and that I did not mean to do this. My mom kept rubbing my head (as she was instructed) and telling me that everything would be okay. She had tears in her eyes but kept herself strong for my sake. My dad, on the other hand, was a mess. He hugged me around my head as best he could and just kept saying that everything would be okay and that he loved me very much. Before that moment, I had never seen my dad cry. When I looked at him that night and saw the tears running down his face, I knew then that this was bad.

My parents got to spend a couple minutes with me before the nurses told them they need to start working on me. I remember them both kissing me on the head and then leaving the room. What happened next is a bit foggy because they had started to sedate me in order to begin to *fix* my body. I do remember someone saying they were going to shave the sides of my head which at the time, seemed devastating. To a teenage girl, their hair is a big part of who you are. So now I was thinking, *Oh my God, I'm going to be an eighteen-year-old with a mohawk!*

Well, it was not quite a mohawk, but they shaved it enough to give the doctor's space to drill on my skull, right above my ears. The doctors inserted bolts that would stick out of my head about an inch. I know it sounds horrific, but it was later explained to me that the bolt was just slightly anchored into my skull bone. A metal curved rod would then be attached to each bolt and went from one bolt, across the top of my head to the other bolt. Through the metal rod was a cord that was attached to fifteen pounds of weight that provided traction on my neck. The traction device was attached to the bed and kept a constant pull on my neck. I spent two months in this bed with the fifteen pounds keeping a constant pull on my neck.

When I was first put into the traction bed, the doctors had thirty-five pounds of weight pulling my vertebrates apart. They would then realized that this was too much weight and would reduce it down. Several hours and four or five X-rays later, they had the traction device at fifteen pounds of weight, and my neck looked good on film. Now the waiting game began. The doctors told my parents that they would wait for the swelling to go down in my spinal cord. I was started on large doses of cortisone through my IVs and was sent up to the Intensive Care Unit to begin the healing process.

I asked my mom what went through her head when they showed her and my dad the X-ray films of my neck, and she told me she wasn't sure if she wanted to throw up or pass out. My mom knew than that my life was now going to be different. She told me that after she saw the X-rays, she closed her eyes and prayed for God to give her the strength to help me handle this. My mom knew she could accept what the future could possibly hold for me.

She could accept any outcome, but she was scared of my reaction.

How was I going to handle this?

Chapter Four

The Party

My Thanksgiving break from school was going by way too fast. It was already Saturday and I had to go back to school on Sunday, which meant back to studying for finals week. I was a freshman at Kent State University and was getting ready to finish my first semester of college.

This holiday break was a big deal at school. It was the first real, long break where we actually had the time to go home. Of course, there had been the long weekend breaks, but this break was finally a *real* break, and I wanted this one to last forever.

Besides being the first real break, this was the time off from school when all my friends who had gone off to different colleges would be home too. So it was an exciting time to be coming home to catch up with all my friends. I was excited to see who loved school, who decided that they maybe wouldn't be going back (because of bad grades or simply because it wasn't for them), or even better, to see who had gained the dreaded Freshman Fifteen (the weight gain that is known to plague most girls their first years of living off of yummy dorm food). So it was an exciting time to be coming home to catch up with all my friends. And yes, if anyone was wondering, I gained the Freshman Fifteen and then some.

I had heard about the party that a good friend was having while I was still at school. This party was going to be for everyone to get together and celebrate the first semester of college coming to an end. I was really excited. On Friday night I had gone out with a group of my friends to the University of Akron bars to get the weekend started, so to speak. There were really no fun hangouts for college kids in my town, and the next closest city with college bars was Akron.

That night, my friends and I hit about three different bars around the University of Akron's campus. We danced, drank beer, and had a great time. I probably had about five beers that night, which, for me, meant I was intoxicated. I somehow drove home from the bars that night and certainly felt my drinking indulgence the next morning.

I woke up the next morning to the phone next to my bed ringing. My first thought as I lay there listening to the phone was, *What was I thinking, drinking so much last night?* My head hurt, my tongue felt like it was a huge, dried out sponge, and the thought of sitting up in bed made me want to vomit in my garbage can. But the phone kept on ringing, and my head kept on pounding louder and louder to the relentless sound.

After several rings, I picked it up, murmured hello, and heard my sister's much too loud voice through the receiver. My sister's voice isn't ordinarily loud, but with a hangover headache, even the smallest noises can sound like thunder. On the other end of the phone, Kimberly voice crashed through my head as she asked me when I was coming over to help her clean her house. My sister was having her first holiday dinner in her home as a married woman, and she wanted everything to be perfect.

Now, I'm going to share something about my sister that she has no idea I'm sharing. She'll know it when she reads it. So here it goes. My sister, as wonderful, loving, and supportive as she is, and I must say that she is my favorite sister (as well as my *only* sister), is not a housekeeper. So, with that said, she most definitely needed my help. Plus, she had asked me in advance. I just didn't know she wanted me to come over at 8:30 a.m.!

So I hung up the phone, rolled out of bed, grabbed my sweat pants and a TaB soda (I loved TaB soda), and off I went. I figured I would shower once I got done helping her so that I would be fresh for the family dinner, and more importantly, the party.

After hours of cleaning, I rushed home, showered, and got myself ready for the night. So I wouldn't need to wear a bulky jacket, I had borrowed a ski sweater from my brother. Jackets were so not cool to wear to a party. Also, it was surprisingly pleasant weather for the end of November in Northeastern Ohio. I knew my brother's sweater would be perfect.

The particular sweater that I had picked to wear was one of his favorites. After agonizing over it, pleading with him, and promising to be super careful with his favorite sweater, he agreed to let me wear it under one condition: I do not, under any circumstance, get anything on it. I thought, *Fine–that was a given. After all, I'm an adult, and really, what could happen to a sweater?*

That night we did the family dinner thing at my sister's (extremely clean) house. My grandmother, great grandmother, and aunt on my mom's side had come in for the holiday weekend from Pittsburgh, so everyone was there. The food was good, and after we all stuffed ourselves, we did the traditional lay-around-the-living-room-watching-television thing.

Looking back at it now, I remember that I almost didn't go to the party because after lying around most of the evening, I became really sleepy and did not feel like fixing myself up again and driving to a party. Knowing this party was going to be awesome, I forced myself out of my comfortable spot on the couch. I freshened up my hair and makeup, said my good-byes to my mom, dad, and grandparents, and off I went. As I was leaving my sister's house, I remember hearing my mom yelling out to me, telling me to be careful and *not* to be late. Of course, I'm sure I rolled my eyes and thought, *Whatever*. I mean, I was in college for gosh sake. At school, we didn't even start going out until 10:30, 11 o'clock at night. Although I respected my parents, I knew they probably wouldn't be up when I get home. And they would have no idea what time it was when I would walk in the door.

As I drove to the party that night, I began to wonder who was still going to be there at that hour. I had hoped to leave my sister's earlier, but it did not work out that way. Besides, I was certain most of my friends would still be there: this was going to be a good party to hang out late.

I arrived at the party around 10 p.m., and it was still going on strong. In my high school days, it was not unusual to show up at a party late as when things were already starting to wind down. If you arrived late to a party, at that point it would be what I like to call a mellow-fest of drunken friends hanging out, maybe listening to music. But not this party. This was a big celebration.

My friend who threw the party was popular throughout high school. I remember going to parties at his house, and they were always a good time. He had a great house for parties, too: a finished basement, nice yard, and plenty of alcohol. And, since we had only been out of high school for less than a year, word about the party spread like wildfire around my old high school, so there were a lot of kids there.

When I arrived at the party, I parked my car on the street with all the others. I remember feeling excited when I saw how many cars were still there – it meant the party was probably still going strong. I walked up the driveway and immediately noticed a group of my old high school friends. They were standing around drinking, smoking, and just hanging out. A friend of mine noticed me walking up the driveway and started yelling my name, and then I remember someone handing me a beer. I started drinking with them, and things just seemed the norm–a bunch of friends hanging out, just having fun, and laughing about old times.

It was shortly after I arrived that one of my good friends informed me that she had gotten a new car. It was her first new-to-her, bought-with-her-own-money car, and she wanted to show it off to her friends. It still had the temporary license plates. She was excited about it and wanted to take me for a ride. Figuring this ride would be like all the other car rides I had gone on before with my friends, I made my way to the passenger seat.

I remember getting into the car, not really thinking anything bad was going to happen. She told me she had taken our good friend Jen for a ride earlier and had a blast, so I was excited to go. What I didn't realize and found out much too late was that Jen actually felt very nervous during this ride. She felt like our friend should not have been driving friends around in her new car.

We backed out of the driveway and onto the street. I really didn't know where we were going, nor did I really care. We were just two old friends going on a ride to see the new car, and this was a time to catch up with one another.

I had been off to college at Kent State University, and she went off into the work world. We were both excited to have some time together, and she was *really* excited to show me her car. We proceeded down the street, catching up and listening to the Prince soundtrack "Purple Rain." The movie had just come out, and it seemed like everyone I knew loved the music. It's funny—the little things we remember.

Since there were a lot of cars parked up and down the street, we were not going very fast. Eventually passing all the parked cars, it was now just a rural, country road. We were talking about the car, college, and our lives when we came to a stop sign at the end of the road.

We sat there for maybe a second or two, looking to see if anything was coming. Knowing it wasn't a high traffic area, she said, "Watch this," and she made a fast turn to the left. We were heading down the center of the street with the car's back end swinging from side-to-side.

I remember grabbing the bottom of my seat and holding on. I thought, *What's going on? This didn't feel right.* I pushed my feet onto the floor of the car as hard as I could to brace myself somewhat. As the car continued down the street, I remember thinking, *What the heck is she doing?* This was supposed to be just a fun, catch-up-on-old-times car ride. As we continued down the center of the road, the car was gaining speed. Looking back on it now, I realize that my friend was trying to get the car back into control, but she simply could not.

The car started into a curve in the road, and as we went into that curve, a car was coming from the opposite direction. In hindsight, I believe the headlights from that car panicked both of us. She then cut the wheel as hard as she could, causing our car to spin in the street. My side then went nose-first into the ditch. The car came out of the ditch, airborne, and went across a driveway, taking out the residence's mailbox. It then went nose-first into the ditch across the driveway, where it flipped end-over-end. It finally came to rest on its roof, sideways in the ditch.

For the most part, I remember her cutting the wheel and the car spinning and then hitting the ditch really hard. I do not remember much of the flipping because it all happened so fast. I remember feeling disoriented and then everything going numb. There was no pain. No screaming. No feeling of broken bones, only numbness. I just lay there. Motionless. *What just happened? Am I dead?*

With the car upside down, my body was thrown into a ball on the ceiling. *What happened? I can't breathe!* I had to force myself to keep breathing. I did not want to die. I thought of my future. Of my goals, my mom, my dad, my sister, my brother, marriage, children... My life. I was eighteen years old. I was *only* eighteen years old. I was not ready to die. I still had my whole life ahead of me, and now it was going to be over. I wanted to just go back in time. I wished I had not gotten in that car. I wished I had not even gone to the party. But it was too late. There was nothing I could do or say now to change what had happen. All that I could do was lie there, motionless, praying– praying that someone got help to us as quickly as possible and praying that everything would be okay.

It seemed like eternity that I lay there before help arrived. I tried to move my arms. I tried to reach for the door handle. I tried to get out of the car. But I couldn't feel them. I could not move them. *Where were they? Do I still have my arms?*

I remember trying to grab my leg with my hand. Trying to feel the texture of my jeans. But I could not feel *anything*. I had to keep breathing. My head felt like it was stuck somewhere because I could feel pressure on it. It felt like it was pinned between the windshield and the dashboard. I later found out that the pressure I was feeling was because the weight of my body was completely on top of my head.

I tried to move my legs, but I could not. What was wrong? I closed my eyes and prayed. I prayed that this

55

was just a bad dream, and at any point, someone was going to get to me and help me out of this car. My arms would then move and work again. My legs would move, and I would be able to feel them. I would be able to breathe. When I opened my eyes up, I saw flashing lights and heard voices. Help was here. Everything was going to be okay now.

The first person to climb into the car and assess me was a police officer. His voice was the voice that gave me comfort, and I thought he was going to make everything better. I remember hearing him say, "Can you hear me?" I tried to get enough breath to force out a response, but all that came out was a whisper. He heard the faint sound and moved in closer and asked me if I could move or feel anything, and I pushed out, "No."

The officer knew the situation was not good. He knew now that I was alive, but if help did not get there soon, I would not be much longer. The officer stayed right there with me, assuring me that everything was going to be okay. Soon an ambulance arrived, and one of the paramedics climbed into the car with the policeman. I remember a gentlemen's voice reassuring me that they would get me out of the car and asking me to remain calm. I was able to tell him, in a whisper, that I couldn't feel anything. He told me everything was going to be okay, and that they would get me out of the car as quickly as possible. I kept saying that I did not want to die and that I did not want to be like the girls on the first floor of my dorm. The kind voice just kept reassuring me that everything was going to be okay. I wanted to believe that it had to be okay.

The paramedics and police officers worked quickly getting me out. Since I was able to tell them I had no movement or feeling, they knew they were dealing with a spinal cord injury. They took every precaution with getting me out.

A large brace was put around my neck to help immobilize my head and neck. They slid a backboard into the car and placed me on it, strapping my arms to my side. They also put two large foam blocks on each side of my head and wrapped tape around my head, the foam blocks, and the backboard. I was totally unable to move my head or neck.

They carefully lifted me out of the car and got me to the side of the road and into the waiting ambulance. At one point when they were getting me out of the car, one of my arms had come unstrapped and was dangling. I remember seeing a gentleman lift my arm back across me. I could clearly see that it was my arm. I recognized my watch and my sweater, but I could not feel his hands on my wrist. I could not feel the motion in my arm and shoulder as he moved it back across my stomach. At that time, I started to panic because I was out of the car and things were *supposed* to be getting better. But they weren't. I just closed my eyes then and kept saying over and over again, "Please God, don't make me paralyzed for life."

Chapter Five

Seventy-Eight Days

If you ask my dad the meaning of seventy-eight days, he would respond by saying that this was the number of days his Barbie spent in Parma Hospital. Seventy-eight days. That is an awfully long time to lie around, which is basically what I did. The traction device that was screwed into my skull in the Emergency Room was attached to the circle bed, making me its prisoner. The circle bed would turn me every two hours from my stomach to my back. This was done so that no sores would develop on the bony parts of my body—shoulder blades, tailbones, elbows, or anywhere that had direct, hard pressure on my mattress. I was not able to move anything. I had tubes in me to go to the bathroom. I had tubes in me for medication. I had to be bathed, dressed, and fed. All that I could do was blink and talk.

Turning me was quite a procedure. A stretcher frame was placed over top of me, and the nurse would screw the stretcher frame to the head and foot of the circle bed. The nurses would then wrap the stretcher frame to the mattress I was laying on with cloth straps, cocooning me in between the two. Once this was complete, the nurse would operate the bed controls to start the actual turning process. I did not like this at all.

I was always stressed about the weights that where hanging from my bed. Keep in mind, those weights hung from the cord, that was attached to the rod, that was attached to the bolts, which had been drilled into my *skull*. When I was being turned, the weights that hung off to the side of the bed were to be guided along the bed during the process. The nurses knew that whatever they did, they were not to lift the weights up while my bed was turning. The whole purpose of the weight was to keep constant traction on my neck. This would keep my vertebrae in good, straight alignment and allow the bone to grow and reattach the vertebrae. If the weight was lifted, there would be no traction on my neck and my vertebrae would compress together. It became standard procedure for me to say while they were turning me, "Just guide the weights, remember?" I would always say this because I feared what would happen if they were lifted.

Well, one evening, my fear became reality. While my mom and dad were still at the hospital (seldom did they leave when visiting hours were over) a new nurse began her shift. She was assigned to take care of me, and when she came in to introduce herself, let's just say that I was less than impressed. She struck me as ditzy and air-headed. Now more than ever, I did not want my parents to go home that night.

Let me interject something here, too. When people spend a lot of time in a hospital, they tend to develop their favorites. They have their favorite staff (including aids and housekeepers), and more importantly, they have their favorite nurses. It's like anything in life, *really*: we all develop relationships with the people we spend the most time with. We learn to love them or despise them. In a hospital it's no different. Favorites become like family.

When my favorites were working, it was somewhat easier for me to let my parents go home for the night. But on this particular night when I had the newbie nurse (she wasn't new to the nursing profession–she was just new to taking care of me), I really did not want my mom and dad to leave. My mom must have sensed my nervousness about my new nurse because, before my parents left that night, she offered to stay and help in the turning of me.

For liability purposes, my mom and dad were not allowed to turn me without a nurse in the room to run the bed controls. My parents could get me completely ready to turn, put the top stretcher over top of me, secure it to the bed, and cocoon me in without a problem. The nursing staff was extremely thankful for the extra help they provided. A nurse would come in, check over everything, and then do the controls. My mom or dad would guide the weight, and all went smoothly. But on this particular night, things did not go smoothly at all. In fact, they turned out very badly.

One of the nurses that had experience with operating the circle bed came in to assist with the turning. The cocooning process was checked over and everything seemed to be in place. The experienced nurse pressed the button to start the turning process, and before I could get my reminder saying out, the newbie nurse had taken the position of guiding the weights. But instead of guiding them, she picked the weights up, holding them as I began to turn.

My fear became my reality, and my neck compressed down. My first thought was to scream out. *My neck, oh my God, my neck!* But thank God, I did not, because she probably would have just dropped the weights. (I can't even think about what that might have felt like or what the outcome could have been.)

Realizing what was happening, the experienced nurse calmly told the newbie nurse to gently release the weights and to just guide them. When the newbie nurse released them slowly, that was when the you-know-what hit the fan. I was crying hysterically. I remember my father flying across the room after the newbie nurse with profanities spewing out of his mouth. Luckily, my mom noticed my father's flight pattern and grabbed my dad before he got to her. If she had not gotten to him in time, there would have been a good chance that the nurse would have needed traction right along with me.

A quick sensory assessment of my body assured the other nurse and my parents that no damage had been done by the lifting of the weights. I never again had that newbie nurse take care of me.

Besides the no-lifting-of-the-weights rule, there were also other issues with turning me. When I was being turned, I would go from lying flat to standing straight up to going down on my stomach, usually all in one smooth turning cycle. When I was in the cycle, I would sometimes experience a little thing called *orthostatic hypotension*, or, simply, passing out. This can happen to a person when they've been lying flat for several days and then they go to the standing position. Basically, there is a change in blood pressure which causes this medical condition to occur.

So when the bed got to where I was upright, I would usually pass out. Not fun. Luckily, my body adapted over time to this change of position, so I would not pass out as much. And I found that if I closed my eyes during the turning and took deep breathes, I would get less dizzy.

Sometimes my mom's job during the turning process was to talk to me. I had a tendency to hold my breath during the turning process. If my mom talked to me and I responded, this assured everyone that I was breathing.

Turning onto my stomach was also another unsetting part of the process. Imagine what it feels like to fall forward and not be able to put out your arms to catch yourself. Although I knew I wouldn't literally fall, that feeling of falling flat on my face was there. Even if I could have moved my arms,which at this point I still could not, they were cocooned to my side. This falling feeling would freak me out. Having my eyes closed helped a little with this part, but that awful feeling never really subsided.

Once I was turned, the mattress that was under me now laid on top of me. The nurses would un-cocoon me and lift the mattress up off my back. Sidearm supports were then attached to the bed, and my arms were placed on them. The mattress would remain attached to the circle bed but up off my backside. This would allow the nurses to check for any sores or bed marks that were starting to develop. And bedsores, as they are called, can develop in an instant.

Thank God I never had any bedsores (knock on wood). I credit this to my mom. She watched my skin diligently, and if an area looked reddened, a foam pad was made with a cutout for my bony part so that the pressure was relived in that area. I remember that my heels where starting to get red one time. Since I could not feel them, I could not say that they were sore. My mom noticed that they were red while I was lying on my stomach, and that same day these lovely blue boots were brought in for me to wear.

My blue booties, as they were called (impressive medical term, I know), had an egg carton look inside of them. This was so my heels would not be directly pressing on a surface. They were not the most attractive boots I have ever worn, but they did the job, and that was all that mattered. I guess this was not one of my times when I was in fashion.

My traction rules were that I lay on my stomach for an hour at a time. I could usually go about two to two and a half hours on my back before the nurses would come in to turn me. While I was on my stomach, my head would rest in a sling-type device. A strap went across my forehead and chin to support the weight of my head. These straps were two springs wrapped with lamb's wool. The straps supported my head, and the fifteen pounds of weight pulled on my head and neck.

After about an hour on my stomach, I would start to develop pain across my forehead from the strap. If my mom and dad were there, I would have one of them stick their fingers between my forehead and the strap. This would give me some relief from the pain and pressure on my head.

When my forehead would start hurting, I knew I was getting close to the end of my hour sentence on my stomach. My mom or dad would start letting the nurses know I was ready to turn back on my back when it closed in on the one-hour mark. This gave the nurses enough time to finish up with their other patients and then make their way back to me. My parents both knew that when the pain started, it was time to notify the nurses.

Once the nurses knew it was time, they would get me turned back over to my back fairly quick. Sometimes, if the nurses were super busy, my mom and dad would get me ready to turn so when the nurse was able to get to my room, she just had to do the bed control. For the most part the nurse usually got in there to do the bed control when the hour was up.

Sometimes, when I was on my stomach, I would scrunch my forehead and the strap across my forehead would move a bit. This would help ease the pain from the strap. One night when my doctor did his medical rounds, I asked him what would happen if the strap across my forehead were to ever slip off. He said that if the strap were to slip off, my head would drop down and my neck would snap, possibly causing death. So, with that known, I would only wiggle my forehead just enough to have the strap move just enough to relieve some pressure.

About five weeks into this "new life," I started to really *not* want to do it anymore. I was tired of trying to move my arms. I was tired of being bathed. I was tired of being dressed and fed. And I was tired of having what they called "range-of-motion" done on my legs. My parents looked tired. My brother and sister looked tired. And why? Because of this whole stupid new world that I had dragged them into. Had I even thought of them when I chose to get into the car that night? Did I think of how a car accident could change their lives? No. I figured if I was ever in a car accident from drinking and driving, it would only be my life that would be affected. I would have to deal with the consequences alone.

While I laid there in the hospital for several weeks, I saw how the consequences of my choice affected all of my family. And I was done. Done hurting. Done being scared of what the future was going to be like. Done of hearing doctors and nurses tell me things would get better. All the dumb clichés that people say when someone is going through hard times—I was done with them all.

One night as I lay on my stomach, I started thinking of my future. I thought about college, marriage, and children. How would I be able to accomplish these things if I'm not like I used to be? As I lay there thinking about everything, my head was starting to feel the pressure from my forehead strap. I began to scrunch my forehead, moving the strap up my head. As I did this, thoughts were racing through my mind—paralysis, life in a wheelchair— and I questioned why I was living. *Why didn't I just die in that car accident?* I thought that if I died, I wouldn't go through any more hell. My mom and dad would not have to go through it. At that point in my recovery, I just wanted to be dead.

My head was really feeling the pressure and discomfort from the strap. I started to call out for the nurses to come turn me back over onto my back but stopped. I could feel the strap slipping farther and farther on my forehead. In my head, I could hear the doctor's voice telling me that if the strap slips off my forehead, "You could die." As the strap kept slipping slowly up my forehead, I remember I was trying to find peace–peace in the fact that my nightmare would be over. I would not have to worry about the future. My mom and dad would no longer have the burden of caring for me. They didn't ask for this. No one–not me or my parents–would be in pain anymore.

As the strap kept slipping and I continued to scrunch my forehead, I heard these words in the back of my mind: *You are only eighteen years old. Eighteen years old.* There was a reason I lived through that car accident. I started to scream out for the nurse, and a bunch of them came running into the room at once. It was very unusual for me to yell out in panic because it wasn't like I was at risk of falling. So when the nurse heard me, the tone of my yelling, they knew something was not right.

As the nurses came through the doorway to my room, I immediately yelled out, "My strap, my strap!" One of the nurses reached under my face, and just as she did that, my forehead strap slipped off my head. The nurse held my head as the other nurses quickly got my bed ready to turn me over onto my back. Once I was returned to my back, I began crying and was scared to death. I was terrified by the thought of how close I had come to ending my life. I then started to cry harder. I knew I did not want to die. I had no idea how hard my fight was going to be to get whatever parts of my body working again, but I knew then that I wanted to live. This didn't mean that there would be no more dark days. Believe me, more of those would come, but I knew beyond a shadow of a doubt that I wanted to live.

Chapter Six

Beginning to Heal

Within days after the strap-slipping-off-my-head incident, a new hospital staff person was assigned to see me. His name was Patrick, and he was a psychologist. Hmmm, go figure. My doctor was apparently concerned that I was not talking enough about my injury. His concern was that I was not dealing with what lay ahead for me in life, so he brought in the shrink. Patrick lasted about two weeks.

Patrick's first day with me wasn't too bad. He asked me general questions about myself, my family dynamics, and where I was in the birth order. He presented me with all the psychobabble questions in the getting-to-know-you part of the assessment (counseling terminology: building rapport). I now understand why he was asking me all of those questions since I myself am in the counseling profession now. But at eighteen, I certainly didn't understand! Although that particular session went okay, I wish I could say the same for the rest.

Patrick's next visit with me started out very much the same. He and I talked a bit about me, but then the testing started. During the second session, Patrick decided we would do some spelling. This would normally not be a problem because I thought I was a good speller. Wrong! I am that person who has to use her index finger to spell. I was a person who would spell in the air or on the fake paper on the tabletop. I now had no movement in my fingers, and I was flat on my back. Without the ability to "write" the words out with my finger, I had to do it in my head. This was going to be a problem.

My first word was *picnic. Okay,* I thought, *this won't be so bad.* I breezed through that word. Next came *museum.* (Just to let you know, spell check corrected this word, because I spelled it wrong.) *Museum* is a word where I really had to think about the letters and what order they appear in. Although there was slightly more thinking involved than with the word *picnic,* I spelled it right. *Whooohooo! Not bad,* I thought. *Two for two.* Patrick did not seem so bad now. But I didn't realize what was to come.

Patrick then suggested, since I was doing well with spelling, that I try some math. If you recall, I mentioned earlier that mathematics is not my strong suit. With hesitant compliance, I said, "Sure." My idea of math and Patrick's idea of math started off the same, but our ideas quickly changed.

We started with basic single-digit multiplication, and this was no sweat. I didn't even need my finger to work it out in the air. I breezed through a couple of these, and then came the mathematical bomb. I remember the equation like it was yesterday. Patrick gave me a word problem. Now I mentioned I was not good with math, right? I cannot overemphasize how much I loathed math. Well, as bad as I was with simple equations, I was two-times worse at word problems. The word problem was this: I am at a store and I see a sweater I like. (Started out good) The sweater is $40. 00. (I'm thinking now, *Okay, not bad, I'm following along with him so far.*) The sweater is 25% off today. (*He lost me.*) How much do you pay for the sweater? (*Now I am done.*)

There were a couple things that were very wrong with Patrick's question. One: I had no idea what kind of sweater it was. Was it acrylic or cotton? Surely it was not cashmere for forty dollars. Two: Seldom did I buy anything on sale, so I never had to figure out sale prices! I'm kidding. Of course I did buy things on sale, but I never calculated the cost. I never knew what the total would be until the sales person rang it up. So with those two strikes against me, I was done.

During these painstaking assessments, Patrick kept writing stuff down in a folder. Sometimes he would just quickly jot something down. Other times it seemed that he was writing a book. It would drive me nuts, because he would never say how I was doing. And I knew that everything he was writing was about me!

It was either during my second or third session with Patrick that I really started to think that there was something wrong with me–not just a broken neck but apparently a broken mind as well!

One morning Patrick came to start our session, and as usual, I was just watching television. He decided that in this particular session, we would start out with spelling again. I said, "Fine, I'm ready." I figured, the quicker we started, the quicker his forty-five minute session would be over, and then it would be time for lunch.

The first word Patrick gave me was something relatively easy, so I started off feeling confident. His second word was *bicentennial*. Seriously, what was this, giving me a spelling word like *bicentennial*! (Thank goodness spell check caught that one.) Without writing that word out in the air, how was I going to manage? I began to panic inside because I knew he was going to write something down. And sure enough, he did.

Patrick just kept it coming. The third word he asked me to spell was *Czechoslovakia*. Hand to God, I am not kidding–Patrick asked me to spell *Czechoslovakia*! (Spell check did its magic on that word just now, too. Although I spelled it wrong, I did give it my best try. Looking back, I should have just said spell C-Z-E-C-H.) And once again,

Patrick wrote more down in his notes. I was never so glad to be done with a session in all my life!

When my parents came to visit me that night after my session with Patrick, as soon as my mom walked through the door of my room, I started crying hysterically. She came right up to my bed and started rubbing my head and kissing my face, asking what was wrong. I managed to get out, between the sobs, that I was upset that she and dad had not told me that I had a head injury. I remember her looking at me with the most confused look on her face as I kept sobbing. I kept sobbing. She looked over at my dad and asked me, "Why on earth would you think you have a head injury?" And through more sobs, I answered back, "Because I cannot spell *Czechoslovakia!*"

I explained further, as she wiped my tears, that during my session that day with Patrick, he asked me to spell *Czechoslovakia*, and I couldn't. I went on to say that I had asked Patrick why I needed to have all these tests done, and that he had told me that there might have been swelling in my brain from the spinal injury.

After I told my parents about this incident, they both busted out laughing. My mom then asked me if I could spell *Czechoslovakia* before I broke my neck. Of course I then realized that I could not spell it even then. She said to me, "What makes you think, Barbara, that breaking your neck gave you the ability to spell it?"

I stopped crying then, and from that day on, I had no more sessions with Patrick. I think my mom must have talked to one of the nurses on duty that night about what had happened during my session. I'm fairly certain a note was put in my chart for my doctor to stop the sessions with Patrick. Even though I still had some really down days, I was thankful that no more therapists came to see me–at least no more at Parma Hospital.

Besides family, nurses, and doctors (of course), I did have a lot of visitors during my stay at Parma Hospital. When I was turned on to my stomach for my hour, anyone who was visiting me then had to lay on the floor on pillows and look up at me.

It was always funny when people would walk by my hospital room during visiting hour and see people lying on the floor on pillows. My mom and dad would tell me that the people would peer into my room with a look on their faces as if to say, "What the heck?"

There was one interesting patient that was a few rooms down from mine. This particular patient had a mental illness, and whenever he would walk the halls at night, he would stop by the doorway of my room. I could see him in my peripheral vision, standing there just starring in at me. Most of the time, when he was doing his nightly "rounds," I would be facing the floor. This gentleman would yell out to the nurses, "Why she got to stare at the floor?" The nurses would then tell him that I was "bad" and that was my punishment. He would then tell them that he promised he would not be bad because he did not want to face the floor. It was our way of having a little fun in this situation.

To help count down the days until I was freed from my "bed prison," we had a calendar taped to the frame of the circle bed. We would mark off the days until I got out of traction. Once I was out of traction, I would then be able to get up in a wheelchair and go down to the therapy departments for my physical and occupational therapy. Up to this point, the therapists had come to my room for my therapy.

Besides wanting to know how many more days I had in traction, it became very standard for me to ask my doctor if I was going to walk again. My doctor quickly caught on to my repetitive question to the point where whenever he came into my room, he would immediately say, "I don't know" before I even got the question out. He would then follow up his answer with the sincere hope that I would and the assurance that with a lot of hard work, prayer, and determination, the sky was the limit for what I could gain back.

One of the questions my doctor did give me a straight answer to was when he planned on taking me out of traction. The day was Monday, January 28th. That made my traction sentencing sixty-five days. For sixty-five days, I lay in bed, face up or face down.

Monday, January 28th was the Monday after the Super Bowl. On Super Bowl Sunday my parents spent all day at the hospital with me because they had been invited to a Super Bowl party that night. My mom had said to me that she and dad would not go if I wanted them to stay with me, but I knew they needed to go. I could see how being at the hospital day in and day out was wearing on them. My parents' daily routine had become something entirely different than it had been before. They would get up in the morning, get ready for work, go off to work, come home, change their clothes, and head up to spend the evening with me at the hospital. They would sometimes not leave the hospital until 10-10:30 at night. My mom said she knew how much it meant to me to have them there, and she and dad would almost always get me ready for bed and to turn onto my stomach. Occasionally, one of them would stay home for the night to do laundry, go through the mail, and pay bills–or rest even. But for the most part, both mom and dad always came.

As much as I wanted them both to stay with me for the Super Bowl that night, I knew they should go to their party. Besides, one of my favorite nurses was on that night, so it would be a better night for me. Not to mention that the following day was the big day, and I would be getting out of traction and free of that bed.

My doctor must have made rounds early that night, because I remember I was watching the Super Bowl game, and it was around nine o'clock. My doctor never made rounds before eleven o'clock in the evening. When he walked into my room so early, it startled me. He asked me, "You ready to get out of that bed?"

I of course responded with, "H-yeah!" He asked me if I was nervous for the next day, getting out of traction, and I said, "Yeah, and I probably won't be able to sleep."

Just then he said, "Well then, let's go ahead and do it now."

Now! Now? I could not even think or say anything. *Seriously, now?* And before I could collect my thoughts, he walked out of the room. Within minutes, my favorite nurse came in, all smiling and asked me if I was excited. *Excited? No. Nervous as heck, yes!* I then told my nurse to call my parents, because they were supposed to be there for this event, but just as I said this, in walked my doctor carrying a big neck brace in his hands. He placed the neck brace on my neck for size and said he liked how it fit. He began to start the process of freeing me from my sixty-five day sentence.

Now let me just say, when the screws that were in my skull were screwed in, I was sedated, and I do not remember a lot. So at this point, I was thinking that the doctor would sedate me to take the screws out. Well, he did not.

I was asking a thousand questions as he was getting everything ready to remove the traction. And just like that, he told the nurse that was helping him to lift up on the weight. *Oh my God, lift up on the weight! No!* The nurse lifted up the weight, and I felt my neck compress down some. My doctor then started unscrewing the one side of the traction device from my skull, and then the other side, and probably within forty-five seconds, the screws where out. I was free!

I did not know what to do. I started to cry, not because I was sad or in pain or anything, but because I think I was just so overwhelmed about what had just happened that the emotions just hit me. Noticing my tears, my doctor asked me why I was crying, and I remember his words: "If you miss the traction device that has been strewed in your head so much, I'll put them right back in."

My doctor was, and still is, a wonderful man. And I am thankful for his humor. I, of course, said, "No thank you," and he bent over and kissed me on the forehead. He told me that it was good that I didn't want them back in because I looked better without the screws. I asked him why he did the procedure that night and not Monday like he planned. I said earlier, my doctor knew me; he told me he knew I would worry about it all night, and this way, I did not get the chance to worry. Boy, did he know me.

Now that I was free, I was put into a "normal" hospital bed. No more having to be cocooned in that frame to be turned. No more forehead strap that gave me such a headache. In a normal hospital bed, I would be able to try to sit up or lay on my side. In my mind, I was thinking that now I would be able to start getting the use of my legs back and getting my fingers to work. Everything looked brighter.

The nurses brought in my hospital bed. Within minutes they counted to three, and with a quick slide on a flat board that they call a sliding board, they slid me over into my new bed. I was now able to see what the whole circle bed looked like. The contraption that I had been screwed to for the last sixty-five days was exactly what I thought, too: it was ugly. But I was very thankful for that bed because it did what it was supposed to do–it helped my neck heal.

Just as the nurses were getting me all adjusted in my new bed, my mom and dad walked in. One of the nurses had called them at their Super Bowl Party and told them that the doctor was taking me out of the circle bed that night. There was no way they were going to get there before my doctor removed the traction from my head, but they wanted to be there soon after.

I was so happy to see them and just kept saying that I could not believe I was free and had got through that experience without them there. Both of them keep saying how proud of me they were and how they couldn't get over how good I looked in a normal bed. My mom could finally lay by my head and love on me without bumping the screw that was screwed into my skull. (When I would be crying or upset, my mom had a tendency to lean on the circle bed and try to hug me around my head. She would kiss my face and tell me everything would be okay. Of course, when she would do this, she would accidentally bump my screw. She would say though that she felt bad.

Now that I was out of the circle bed, I could really start working hard on getting the use of my body back. I was ready.

Chapter Seven

Rehab

My parents had talked to the doctor and the social worker at Parma Hospital about where would be the best place for me to get better and continue to heal from this injury. The social worker gave them several options: Craig Rehabilitation Hospital in Colorado, Dodd Hall in Columbus, and Edwin Shaw Rehabilitation Hospital in south Akron. My parents immediately ruled out Colorado because of the distance. They both knew how important it was to me to have the two of them close to me throughout this recovery.

They did research on Dodd Hall, and after all was said and done, they both felt Edwin Shaw would be the best for me because of its proximity and rehabilitation quality. The social worker had told my parents that recovery was not only physically hard but also emotionally and mentally hard. Since Nov. 25th, my parents had only missed about three days of my recovery. With that said, my parents knew that I was going to need them more than ever during this next stage.

On February 11th, 1985, I was transported by ambulance from Parma Hospital to Edwin Shaw Rehabilitation Hospital. Since I could not sit fully upright in a wheelchair, insurance required that I be transported via ambulance. My mom had spent packing up my hospital room of all the thousands of gifts, cards and stuffed animals that I had received over the last seventy-eight days. She loaded up her car with everything and would follow the ambulance to my new residence for the next stage.

I remember that as they were loading me into the ambulance that day, I said to one of the attendants that I had not been outside since the end of November. Seventy-eight days inside a room; that sounds more like a punishment than recovery. But, boy, it felt good to breathe in the cold February air that morning.

I had no idea what to expect when I arrived at Edwin Shaw Rehabilitation Hospital. One thing I did expect was that this would be the place that I would walk out of. I had hoped it would have been from Parma Hospital, but since that did not happen, no big deal. I would just walk out of here.

The doctor in charge of Edwin Shaw Hospital was Dr. Grotz. Dr. Grotz was a physiatrist, which is a doctor specializing in rehabilitation medicine. He had come to see me at Parma Hospital to determine if I qualified for rehab at Edwin Shaw. I remember thinking the first time I saw him, *My God, he's old!* He was probably in his sixties, but I remember he had white hair and walked really, really fast.

At Parma, Dr. Grotz did a full physical assessment on me. Afterwards, he told my parents that he felt I would be a good candidate for the rehabilitation department at his facility. He went on to tell them that as soon as they had a bed available, I could be admitted.

During my assessment, I had asked him how long he thought I needed to be there until I would be back to normal and walking again. His response was four to six months, with no promises on the outcome–which meant there was no promise I would walk again. He went on to say that the outcome would be up to me and how hard I wanted to work in rehab. To me that was easy enough. I was planning on working super hard to get over this injury and back to normal, everyday life.

When Dr.Grotz left after his assessment on me, my mom, dad, and I discussed all that he went over. All three of us felt that Edwin Shaw would be the best fit for the next stage of this recovery. My mom had heard how good Edwin Shaw Hospital was, and she thought Dr. Grotz's assessment of me was very thorough. With my mom as a nurse, my dad and I both relied strongly on her and her medical knowledge throughout this entire process. My mom knew all the big medical words that doctors were spewing out, confusing me and my dad. My dad and I would just stare with that deer-in-the-headlights look when the doctors started talking with their highfalutin terms. With that said, whatever mom believed was good for me, my dad and I went along with it.

I arrived at Edwin Shaw in the late morning on February 11th and moved into a room at the end of the hall on one of the rehabilitation floors. It was an old building that was once a tuberculosis hospital. They added on to the old hospital, and the part that I was in was the newer part.

My room was not bad for a rehab hospital room. It did not have the typical hospital room (not that I had been in many rehab hospital rooms before this) feel or look. It had nice artwork (at least as nice as you can get for a rehab room). My room was on the second floor, and the unit was right across from the cafeteria, which worked out good for when mom and dad came to have dinner with me. There was one thing I did not like about my new digs: I had a roommate.

At Parma, I was in a private hospital room. That was really nice because my mom and dad could stay later than the usual visiting hours. We would just shut the door and nobody knew that they were still visiting. Not that any one of the nursing staff at Parma Hospital would have ever said anything. When my parents stayed later than the normal visiting hours, my mom would get me totally ready for bed, freeing up the nurses to do all their other duties.

Basically, the nurses at Parma loved having my parents there, but we were not in Parma Hospital anymore, Toto!

My roommate was a little old lady named Mary. And by old, I mean old. Ms. Mary was probably in her late eighties, early nineties, and was in rehab for a broken hip. Apparently, she had fallen at home and broken her hip and was now at Edwin Shaw to get back on her feet again. She was there for pretty much the same reason I was there– minus the broken hip and add in a broken neck– but basically, we had the same expected outcome in my mind.

Ms. Mary was a sweet woman, don't get me wrong, but she was a bit of a complainer. Since I was coming from a private hospital room to now having a roommate, her complaining was a bit of an adjustment. Mary would continually moan throughout the day and repeatedly cry out, "Nurse, I am dying." After about a week or so of this moaning and crying out, I found myself saying to myself, *Would you die already... I need to get some sleep!* That sounded non-empathetic (which I am very empathetic!). But Mary not only moaned and cried out during the day, but also all though the night as well. Because of her crying and moaning, I was not able to sleep. Since my days were filled with therapies, I needed sleep more than ever.

After about two weeks, a private room opened up across the hall from our room, and I was moved over there. I could still hear Mary faintly, but the nurses would pull my door almost shut; therefore, I was finally able to sleep.

My days at Edwin Shaw were much more exhausting than my days at Parma. At Parma, I lay in an ugly bed and got fed, bathed, and turned. At Edwin Shaw, things were different. My days quickly became filled with occupational therapy (OT), physical therapy (PT), and rec (recreational) therapy. I would have OT and PT in the morning, usually an hour each, and then I would go back up to my unit for lunch. In the afternoon, it was back down for about an hour and a half of PT, then maybe an hour of OT again. Rec therapy was usually just twice a week. By the end of the day, I would be physically spent.

My dad would always come spend the evenings with me because his office was maybe fifteen minutes away. There were a lot of nights when dad would just come from work. This way my mom could then go home after working. This set-up worked well because it gave my mom the chance to get caught up on everyday chores around the house.

My first day going to therapy was not fun. On therapy days, a volunteer would take patients who were scheduled for therapy. The therapy departments were located in the basement of the old part of the hospital. The volunteer would push the patient to the gym area, where they would line all of them up in their wheelchairs like cars waiting for service.

The therapy departments were located in the basement of the old part of the hospital, and a volunteer pushed patients there who could not take themselves. The PT gym was a big open room with standing tables, parallel bars and low tables with mats on them. There was equipment hanging on the walls–pulleys with weights on them that people could manipulate from their wheelchairs. There were walkers, standing platform walkers, walkers with wheels, walkers with tennis balls for feet–basically tons of stuff that looked totally scary and foreign to me.

I remember I was excited about getting into therapy and starting to really work hard on getting my body to work again. I thought that the quicker I got started with this therapy thing, the quicker I would get back to walking again–back to my old life! But part of me was terrified, too. I had no idea what to expect. To be honest, I figured, *Well, I learned to walk once already in my life. How hard can it be to learn it again? Besides, I'm older now, so it will be like a refresher course of what I learned as a toddler.*

My first day in the therapy gym was hell! I could not do a thing for myself. I could not sit up unsupported. I could not push my arms down on the mat and scoot my butt over on the mat. I could do nothing! Yet, I was exhausted by the time it was over! I would have sworn by the level of my exhaustion that I had just run ten miles and done a hundred push-ups. Yet, in reality, all I had done was try to transfer myself from my wheelchair to an elevated mat table...With three people helping me!

As the days went on and the weeks went by, I did get stronger. Instead of three people assisting me in moving from my wheelchair to the mat, I eventually got down to two people. I would still be exhausted, but I could feel myself getting stronger. This was good.

From physical therapy I would be wheeled over to the occupational therapy room. The goal of occupational therapy was to focus more on strengthening my arms and hands and getting them to wake up and remember what they were supposed to be doing.

I would usually spend an hour in OT lifting weights, stacking cones, and getting electrical stimulation done to my forearm muscles. The purpose of the electric stimulation was to give my arm nerves a zap, so to speak, to hopefully wake them up.

My PT therapist was named Donna and my OT was Bonnie. The two of them were incredible, and by the end of my stay at Edwin Shaw, I had become close friends with them both. Donna and Bonnie would work me hard and push me when I felt like I could not do any more reps. I remember lying on the mat after this grueling transfer from my wheelchair to the mat table, and I just started sobbing. She and I ended up just laying there the whole therapy hour, and she let me cry. She reminded me that it was going to be hard and not to get down and discouraged. I owe her so much for letting me cry that day and encouraging me to fight on.

Bonnie was equally as awesome as Donna when it came to letting me cry when I needed to. Bonnie and I would start my therapy sessions by doing range-of-motion on my arms and shoulders. She and I would be talking about everything there was to talk about during my therapy, from soap operas to hot guys.

A perfect example of our closeness is when I would come in OT feeling down, Bonnie would pick up on my mood. (It was probably a mom thing.) She would take me across the hall to one of the smaller OT workout rooms, shut the door, and the waterworks would hit. She too would sit with me and tell me that she knew it was hard, but I could do it.

Bonnie had been an OT for a long time and had worked with all kinds of injuries. She saw people struggle and sweat to move their wrist one millimeter. And when the person did this tiniest movement, she would be just as happy and excited as if she had just accomplished it. So I knew Bonnie knew—both physically and emotionally—what recovery felt like.

Bonnie's job was to get me as independent as possible with my hands and arms. She made adaptive braces for my hands and wrists to help me pick up things or to hold a toothbrush. She would have me stacking cardboard cones as high up as I could go. This exercise helped me strengthen my shoulders, along with my stomach and back muscles. Bonnie was constantly thinking of new ways for me to work out my upper body.

During all these exercises, I would be thinking to myself, *when is it all gonna kick in and my body start to work again?* How could a body that worked perfectly fine for eighteen years all of a sudden forget how to work? In one second!

Over the weeks of therapy, my body did get stronger, and I was slowly learning to be more independent. The key word there is slowly. I had learned to feed myself with the braces Bonnie made for my wrist and hands. This was huge! I don't know about anyone else, but I am sure the only good time for someone to feed someone else is when one of them is an infant. I hated being fed! There, I said it. (Boy does that feel good!) But it still was not how I used to eat. So the struggle emotionally was getting harder.

There would be days, or weeks even, where there was no improvement. I would not feel like I was getting stronger. I was not making huge gains in my strength, and my progress was slowing down. The therapists and doctors would assure me that this was normal for spinal injuries and that patients can have huge gains in both movement and the senses, while other times they could have minimal gains. I was told then that I could be reaching a plateau in my recovery (this is what they call a leveling out in a person's recovery) and that I should not worry.

I should not worry, I remember thinking. That's easy for them to say as they stand there on their two good working legs! I should not worry. Hells to the yeah I should worry! I was still in a flipping wheelchair, unable to use my hands or legs or take myself to the bathroom! Bull larkie, don't worry! I wanted to be better by now. I wanted to be walking. That was my plan.

It was at that time, maybe four to five months into my recovery, that I came to realize that *my* timeline of recovering and my *body's* timeline of recovery were not in sync. I realized at that time that this recovery was going to be long, with no guaranteed outcomes. All the things Dr. Grotz had said to me back when I was at Parma Hospital were now coming into reality. I now had to learn to get my mind and body to work on the same timeline. That was not an easy thing to do.

Basically, what I had to learn to do at that point was to get an eighteen-year-old mind to learn to be patient with about an eight-month-old body. Think about that! When we are babies learning to walk, our cognitive development is moving along at the same pace as our physical development. We don't know any better because we don't know what we don't know, right? At eight months old, we don't know that we should be feeding ourselves or getting dressed by ourselves, let alone walking! But when we are eighteen years old, or 216 months old (for those parents who say that their kids are 30 months old instead of 2 ½ years old... Really?), you know what you should be doing physically. It was very hard to get a normal, working mind to accept and work with a broken body.

So, Monday through Friday I would spend mornings and afternoons in therapy. On the weekends, my family and some friends would come to visit me at the hospital. Like at Parma Hospital, my parents very rarely missed a day coming to see me, and when they could not come, friends of my parents would.

I had been at Edwin Shaw for months when the team of therapists and doctors decided it would be good for me emotionally to go home for a day pass. I was ecstatic! I had not been home since the night of my accident, and it had been at least seven months since the accident. I remember being so excited when they told me about the pass. I was finally going to be able to go home. I did not care that it was for only for eight hours or so–I was going home!

The week prior to me going home for my first day pass was like waiting for Christmas. It seemed like the weekend would never come. When the day did finally arrive, I was up and dressed early, ready to get out of there. The aides that took care of me knew how excited I was, so I was the first patient they bathed and dressed that morning. I had to be transported by ambulance because I was still not allowed to sit up in a vehicle (insurance stuff), but I so did not care. At that point, I would have converted to being Amish and ridden home in a horse and buggy! Having to ride in an ambulance again was fine with me because I was going home.

The drive home took forever. I remember just laying there staring out the back window of the ambulance, wondering how much longer until we arrived. The driver of the ambulance told me when we were on my road, and I remember thinking, Home! It feels so good to be going home! It was not how I had planned on going home for the first time. My plan had been to be walking when I went home, but I had time still to make that happen. I was just glad to be out of hospitals and home.

The ambulance pulled into my parents' driveway, where they unloaded me and wheeled me around to the back of the house. Some of my parent's friends had built a ramp onto the back patio of the house and another ramp to get me in to the family room. Once they got me into the family room, my mom transferred me from the ambulance gurney to my wheelchair, which mom and dad had brought in the car. I remember looking around the family room and thinking everything looked pretty much how it looked months ago when I was last there. Not much had changed. My dog, Brandy, jumped right up onto my lap and gave me many kisses on the face. Thank God he was a poodle and not a Labrador.

The ambulance workers left, but not before my mom scheduled my ride back to Edwin Shaw. I remember my mom telling them to be back around seven so that we could get back to the hospital by eight that night. We were given a list of rules when we left the hospital, and one specifically said all patients needed to be back by eight! Since this was my first pass out of the hospital, my parents followed the rules. I remember I didn't care what time my mom told the ambulance to be back to get me–I was home!

That visit was awesome! After spending several hours in my wheelchair sitting with all the guests who came to see me, my mom and dad moved me to the couch, where I sat for a couple of hours. Pillows had to be propped all around me to keep me from falling over. At that point in my recovery, my abdominal muscles had not yet kicked in, so sitting without the security of my wheelchair to provide support was not very stable.

My parents had to learn how to move and transfer me before I was allowed to go out on a pass. They were required to learn the technique used to transfer me from my wheelchair to somewhere else. It helped that my mom was a nurse because that gave the hospital staff more assurance that I would be fine while I was on home visits.

After sitting on the couch for a while and getting all kinds of loving from Brandy, my mom and dad transferred me back into my wheelchair for the rest of the visit. I really think my dad liked when I was out of my wheelchair just sitting on the couch, because I looked like "the old Barb." Me just sitting on the couch and talking was normal. It was enjoyable for all of us.

I always wanted those home visits to go by super, super slow. I never wanted to go back to the rehab hospital, but I knew I had to go back to keep getting stronger and conquering this injury. Still, it never got easier leaving home to go back there.

Chapter Eight

The New Normal

When I went into Edwin Shaw Rehabilitation Hospital on that snowy February day, I expected, or at least thought, I was going to leave there like the old Barb–a very active person, a cheerleader, the girl always on the go. And most importantly, the girl who could walk. All the therapies were supposed to get me back to the old Barb. All the range-of-motion on my arms and legs, all the lifting of weights was going to jar my muscles and body back into remembering what it was supposed to do. I mean, come on, my body was perfectly normal for eighteen years; how can that all change in one second?

What I did not know during the time I spent in rehab was that my life *would* go back to normal, but not the normal I had remembered or was used to. It would be a *new* normal. And it was going to take a long time for my eighteen-year-old mind to accept the new ways of my new life.

I can truly say now that I understand the saying, "You do not know what you have or appreciate what you have until it is taken from you." Whether it is a person, a thing, or *anything* that takes root in our hearts and is suddenly taken away from us. We miss it every day and want it back so bad. And yes, we go through the "what ifs." What if it was me that had gone out to the store instead of them; what if I had communicated more and said I love you more; or in my situation, what if she had turned right onto that road instead of turning left?

As a person goes through the "what ifs," in the end we have to come to terms with the fact that it is *not* going to come back. And it is at this crossroad where we can find ourselves saying, "Why me? This is not how I saw my life, and it was not supposed to happen to me." I said those two words a lot: *why me*. On my darkest days, I would cry them out. There were many points throughout this recovery that my life had more darkness in it than light. This relentless injury and the recovery had taken all the joy from my life, and I desperately wanted my old life back.

As the days went by, I continued to get stronger in my upper body. Bonnie, my occupational therapist, would come to my room in the morning and work with me on getting myself ready for the day. She would come in with all kinds of splints, wash clothes that were made to look like mittens, and thick-handled toothbrushes for me to use to try to become more independent in my ADLSs, or active daily living skills.

ADLS is a medical term used quite often in the rehab setting, and those familiar with rehabilitation would know exactly what the acronym ADLS means. I found out rather quickly that if I couldn't get a hold of these medical acronyms early on in my recovery that it was quite possible that I would develop a severe anxiety disorder. I would hear these acronyms and start to think that these so-called letter words could be a new test that they were going to do on me, or worse, it could be a setback in my recovery.

So it was at some early point in my recovery that I realized not only did I have to adjust physically and emotionally to the change in my life, but I also was being subliminally forced to learn a new language. A person is literally thrown into a bowl of alphabet soup of medical acronyms. For instance, UTI (urinary tract infection), PT (physical therapy), OT (occupational therapy), SCI (spinal cord injury), and I could go on and on and on. But you get my point, I'm sure. And if a glossary or handbook on what these terms mean is not given out during the early stages of recovery, a person could be seriously overwhelmed. But again, I will say, *Thank You God!* for a mom that was, and still is, the best nurse ever!

Back to the part of Bonnie and getting ready in the mornings. Bonnie would come up to my room a couple of mornings a week and show me new ways of getting myself ready in the morning. First, we would start with bathing.

Bonnie would put the wash mitten over my hand, and a Velcro strap secured the mitt to my wrist. The mitt was strapped to my wrist because I could not grip or grab the wash mitten.

I would wash my face, neck, and as much of my upper body as I could. Bonnie would stand by my bed and guide my arm to the area I would be trying to reach. She needed to do this because I did not have good arm control. Once I had soaped up the area on my body I was washing, I would dip my wash mitt into the washbasin to rinse it. Since I could not wring out the wash mitt very well, by the time bathing was over, the bed and I were both drenched. Bonnie would humorously note at the end of the bath workout that we would need to work on the wringing part a little more. I would always second that motion.

After bathing would come the club-handled toothbrush device, which I am sure could be used as a weapon. Brushing my teeth was huge on my things-to-learn-quickly list, and oh, by the way, in case you were wondering, walking was at the top of this list. I was so excited about learning this newfound independence—brushing my own teeth never felt so good.

I am very proud to say that I did very well in "Tooth Brushing 101" class with Bonnie, and from that point on in my recovery, I brushed my own teeth. Baby steps, I guess.

Looking back on that accomplishment now, every time I brush my teeth today, which is two-to-three times a day (in case my dentist reads this), I always think about how long I could not do the activity. Again, this was something I took for granted and did not appreciate–this simple task of teeth brushing. A task that people do every day without thinking–until it was taken away.

Next came learning to dress independently, or as independently as I could. To start, I had to learn how to dress my upper body. First would be my shirt. I would get my arms in the armholes of my shirt with quite a bit of pulling and tugging with my teeth (thank God, I could brush them, and they were clean!) Once I got the shirt to where my hands were sticking out of the armholes, I would stretch with my arms and pull with my teeth till the shirt was for the most part all the way up my arms. Now came the interesting part–I now needed to get the shirt over my head. No big deal, right? Well, I would quickly find out that yes, it was a big deal, as I had limited ability to lift my arms up over my head. And keep in mind, all while I am doing this motion, I am trying to stay sitting upright. It takes a lot of core abdominal muscles to do even the simple task of putting on a shirt.

Throughout all these daily living skills that Bonnie and I would attempt each morning, Bonnie's job was to be there to assist me if needed. So, when I would struggle to do activities like dressing myself, brushing my teeth, and fighting to get into a t-shirt, Bonnie would just stand-by. Remember, her job was to help me become as independent as possible. I am very thankful *now* for her standing by as I was struggling, but at the time I was learning or relearning I should say, to do these things...I would rather not say how I felt. Let us leave it at that.

But again, baby steps. And sure enough, the more I did these activities myself, the more proficient I became. It was now starting to be normal to do these things this way. I was finally finding my *new* normal.

I forgot to mention this a little ways back: putting on my shirt was great when it was warm out. Basically, I would wear a t-shirt, so putting on a t-shirt was fairly easy to do. But as we Northeastern Ohioans know, summer and warm temperatures are short-lived in this neck of the woods. So when the temperature fell below seventy-five degrees, I was freezing.

One thing I found out about SCI, (you remember what that is, right?) is that it is not uncommon for spinal cord injured people to constantly be cold. The reason is this: We are not up moving around, so our blood is not circulating to keep our bodies warm. As a result, when it got cooler out, I was freezing all the time.

What I found to be my new best friend in the cool months were turtleneck sweaters. So, out would come the turtleneck sweaters. Putting a t-shirt on by myself was a piece of cake; a turtleneck sweater, on the other hand, was a whole new ball game. Let me just say I would have done fine if I never wanted to see where I was going or if I was out to rob a bank or something. But since seeing was something I really enjoyed and robbing a bank was not on my bucket list, I needed to figure out how to get the turtleneck part of the sweater off my face.

So, using my wrist to pull the fabric down my face, I managed to free my face and would then push the turtleneck down with my chin. I remember thinking to myself, either this better get easier quickly or I am moving to a warm climate and joining a nudist colony.

As I learned my *new* way of doing things in order to not let this stupid injury win, remembering how I used to do things was never far away in my thoughts. Even today when I think about the ways I did things before my injury compared to how I do things now, I think the biggest thing that stands out in my mind is that people do not think about *how* they are doing these activities. We take doing these activities for granted.

As the months passed by, I would have my good days and my bad days. When the bad days would roll in (no pun intended here), they seemed to stick around for a while. Similar to my experience at Parma Hospital, the nights were the hardest to handle emotionally. During the day, I would be busy with therapy. I was working so hard that the days would go by quickly. But at night, when mom and dad had gone home and I was in bed watching television, my mind would go on overdrive. I had nothing to distract my mind from thinking as I lay in bed at night, *why me?*

I remember so many nights lying there thinking that this could not be real. Thinking to myself that no way is this *my* life. *Why me?* I remember looking at my hands, looking at my fingers, and remembering all the things they used to be able to do. When would they remember how to do all those things again? That was a question I found myself asking over and over again in my head: *When was everything going to go back to normal?*

I would ask every chance I got, "When will my body return back to normal?" All the responses would be the same–no one knew, but they all would follow this saying with, "But Barb, you *will* make it." So I would hold on to those words, I *will* make it. But those words did not stop my mind at night going to old thoughts and memories of how my life used to be.

One good thing about the nighttime was that it would be a time to go to sleep and dream. And dreaming was good. I found that when I would dream, I never dreamt that I was paralyzed. I always dreamt that I was walking. I still do today. So, after I was prepped for bedtime by the nurse's aides and I was in bed for the night, I would want to fall asleep quickly so that I could return to being *normal.*

Chapter Nine

Acceptance

A full recovery is what everyone hopes and prays for when traumatic situations occur in a person's life. It was not until several years into this life-changing experience that I started to think that maybe there was not going to be a full recovery from this injury. I wanted to hope and believe that I would have a full recovery from this tragic event, but it does not always how we hope. People would send encouraging saying and prayers throughout my stay in the hospitals which would help tremendously to keep my spirits up, but then days would go by, then weeks, and reality would start to sink in. Sometimes, we do not have control of our reality. Sometimes, bodies do not make full recoveries, and sometimes, lives do not go back to normal. Now that becomes our reality. So what comes next is acceptance.

When I remember having a problem in my life, my first thought was to fix it. Let me define "a problem" by saying a circumstance that threatens my wellbeing. So, by fixing it, I mean making the problem go away. That would happen either by ignoring it and hoping it went away on its own or basically getting rid of the problem. (Not that I killed anyone or anything... Not get rid of it like that!) That was how I would handle a problem in my life. However, this life problem of mine was not going away.

I remember the poor-me times. *Why was this happening to me? What have I ever done in my life to deserve this?* I would be thinking to myself that I did not deserve to go through this pain and that there were way worse people out there that deserve this life sentence. And that is what this injury is—a life sentence, a life sentence with no chance of parole. So I could choose to accept this life or hope it would get fixed soon.

There are steps a person has to go through when they are moving towards acceptance. At first, a person wants to blame someone or something for what has happened to them. I wanted to blame someone, anyone, for this happening to me. I was into the self-pity stage of the recovery. If I accepted *my* responsibility for this injury, I would then have no reason to feel sorry for myself, and at this stage of acceptance, I simply was not ready to accept that part.

It took me a long time to accept *my* responsibility and realize that this life-changing event was my fault. However, I wanted to be angry with the girl who was driving the car that night. I even wanted to be angry with my friend who had the party that night. *Why did he have to have so much alcohol at the party? Why didn't any of my friends there try to stop us from going on that ride?*

One thing I had to realize over time was that it was no one's fault but my own. I got into that car that night on my own will, and I had to accept my responsibility in choosing to go for that ride. Trying to blame someone for the way things had turned out did not change the fact that my life was what it was. I had to learn that going through life angry and bitter or having the poor-me attitude was not going to change things. I had to accept *my* responsibility for my life-changing choice and decide to move beyond the consequences of my choice. That was easier said than done.

Accepting my responsibility was hard. It took seven years to be able to not feel anger anymore and to forgive.

I did not always show my anger and self-pity outwardly to everyone. More often I held it inside, letting it consume me. I would share my angry feelings with my family and those really close to me, but for the most part, I held them inside. Why? Because I think deep down inside I knew whose fault it was. I knew I should be angry with myself and hate the way my life was because of my choices, but I just did not want to accept it. I figured, if I just kept suppressing those feelings and put all my effort into getting better, no one would have to accept anything and life could go back to normal.

Besides suppressing my feelings, I would distract my thoughts. When my friends came to visit me, it created a good distraction, but sometimes I found myself "back in my head." I would watch how their bodies moved, and I would watch how they crossed their legs or used their hands. I would almost study every movement that they made with their bodies. As my friends and I would be visiting and talking about the life going on outside of the hospitals, in my mind, I would be thinking, *do they even realize the muscles they are using to cross their legs or the amount of work it takes for them to move their fingers?* I would keep thinking that my body would work again that way. Someday my hands and fingers would move the way my friend's hands and fingers moved.

The one-year anniversary came and went, and I had figured I would have been walking by then for sure. If not walking, at least I would have full use of my upper body and hands. But since I did not, I figured it would be soon after. At this point, I still did not think to myself or believe that this new way of life was going to be permanent. I truly believed that I was going to get better; it was just going to take a little longer.

My daily mantra at that time became, "Don't get frustrated Barb, it will get better." I would just keep saying that over and over in my mind when I would get frustrated. Remarkably, there were days when it would work and I would push forward, but the dark days were still present. And those days could creep up quickly.

It was usually when I would have several dark or down days that people would say to me that in time things would get easier. My response to them would be, "Okay, when?" I remember being tired of being patient. And I remember being *done* with waiting to see what was going to get stronger on my body and what had plateaued out.

When I would be having a good day, my thoughts would be that this whole thing was not that bad because it was just temporary. The good days usually occurred when I would have really good days in therapy and my body seemed to be starting to wake up. Maybe a finger would show some sign of movement, maybe a flicker of a muscle. This incredibly small movement would make me think, *okay, things are starting to come around.* But then, all of a sudden, I would get hit with sadness and anger, and the dark days would creep back in.

On dark days, I would go through the motions of therapy and suppress my sadness. I knew when my parents got there in the evenings that I could cry. I could cry and be angry and want to come home, and they would hold me and say everything was going to be okay. My parents would reassure me that I was continuing to get better and that I needed to be patient. For that moment, it did seem to get better. But at night, after my parents had left and I was alone in my hospital room, I would become overwhelmed with the whole thing again and start crying more. I would cry and say, *why me?* I would feel that I could not do it anymore. I could not be patient anymore.

Through faith I found acceptance. Patience was a word that I remember hearing all the time throughout this recovery. Everyone would say to me, "Just be patient, Barb. God gives you nothing that you cannot handle." Or, I would get the saying, "Good things come to those who are most patient." Well, one can only imagine my thoughts on these sayings over time—let's just say they were not nice thoughts. If God was giving me something that He thought I could handle, He and I never really *talked* about what I could and could not handle, so I was a little upset, to say the least, with God at that time.

Growing up, religion was not a huge priority in our home. My parents believed in God and my siblings and I were raised to believe there was a God, but as far as going to church or Sunday school to worship? That all ended when my mom started working nights when us kids were little and my dad was left in charge of taking us kids to church. Can you imagine a father in charge of getting three small children ready for church? I am sure there are many men out there that can and do. My father, however, was not one of those men.

It was in the early weeks of my injury that I accepted Jesus as my Savior and trusted in Him to help me get through this. Without faith or the support of people around us that care, we will struggle when a traumatic situation happens. In order to learn how to accept what has happened and overcome a life-changing situation in our lives, I believe having faith is key.

Acceptance, for me, was the only real way to move from despair and anger from this injury to tranquility and peace in my life. Oh, sure I was still going to have the poor-me days and the why-me times, but that's called life. And life does have to go on, so I had to learn to live with consequences and the way life was now. Until we accept the outcomes of life's unexpected events, we cannot move forward.

I don't want to say that I surrendered to my injury, because when I think of the word surrender I think that surrendering means to lose or give up. I do not think my injury won over my life or that I gave up trying to recover from this injury. But by using the word surrendering, I surrendered to the fight of not accepting the outcome of this injury, and doing this allowed me to see that there still is a life to live. It took seven years for me to see this, but I still had a life ahead of me.

When I decided to accept the way my life was now, not only did I have to deal with my own emotions and feelings but also the emotions, feelings, and thoughts of all those that were so close to me throughout this recovery—my family and close friends. At first, I felt like I had let them down by not making a full recovery from this injury. I remember thinking to myself, *what would my father think if I cannot walk again? Would he think that I did not try hard enough to recover fully, and only if I had just done more therapy and had tried harder, I would have gotten better?*

It was very hard emotionally to imagine what people would think if I never walked again. And believe me, there is no one on this earth that wanted to and still wants to walk again more than me. I wanted the old Barb back. But again, having the wisdom to see and realize that life was never going to be the old way helped move me through how I thought others would feel.

I can't say that something magical happened to me that made me accept my new life, but I just did. Instead of being angry and depressed and saying *why me* the rest of my life, I started to appreciate what I still had. I could still breathe on my own. I could still talk and move my arms and feed myself. I had to *learn* to enjoy what I still had. I was alive.

Yes, my life was going to be different, but I was alive. Do I wish I never broke my neck? Hells to the ya I do! I would think about this too. I remember for the longest time wishing I had just broken a leg, or heck, both legs. A person recovers from broken legs. I remember thinking, *heck, I could handle having to recover from two broken legs.* My life would have gone back to normal after maybe six or seven months. There was even a time when I had wished I had broken my back instead of my neck and was paralyzed from the waist down. Had I broken my back, I would at least have had the full use of my arms and hands. What I had to realize was that "wishes" and "what ifs" were not going to get me anywhere. What they were doing though was preventing me from seeing what I could still do for myself. When I finally stopped wishing and what if-ing, I was able to see that there was still a lot of enjoyment left in my life. I started to live again.

When I finally accepted the consequences of a decision that I had made in my life, I was able to find peace. It was at that same time in my recovery that a very, very wonderfully dear friend of my family gave me a picture. This wonderful family friend was my Aunt Pat. Aunt Pat was not a blood-related aunt to me, but she was as close and precious to me as any blood relative. The picture that Aunt Pat had given me had a prayer painted on it that said, "GOD grant me the Serenity to accept the things I cannot change; Courage to change the things I can; Wisdom to know the difference." I remember looking at that painting every day throughout my recovery, reading it and rereading it, and thinking, *what does it all mean? How does any of that apply to my situation?* What I later came to realize and accept was that when I finally accepted my life and had faith, God was with me. It was through faith and family support that I learned to accept the things in my life that were not going to change. I later learned that this prayer painting that my Aunt Pat had given me was the Serenity Prayer, and I live by it to this day.

I could not change what had happen to me. Yes, I could wish it never happened, but I could not change it. It was through faith that I learned to accept my life and move on. I could now see that my true strengths within myself where not physical strengths but emotional and spiritual strengths. The goal in my life up to the night of my injury was to enjoy life to the fullest and worry about the consequences of enjoying life later. Enjoying life to the fullest and having happiness before my crash involved destructive decision-making for me. Through faith, I learned that having true life happiness came in knowing God and having Him in my life.

I would be lying if I said I never think about what it would be like to be walking or what it would be like to be independent with my personal care. By accepting my life as a person with a disability, I have been able to move on and live a very happy life. That does not mean I have stopped thinking about being able-bodied person again. I will probably always think about that in the same way that a person who loses someone close to him or her still thinks about that person. A person will always miss what is gone from their life. They will think about the person or thing and dream about it. That is actually normal. Look, the word normal actually can be used still!

What I have come to learn and witness in life is that no two people are alike. How or when one person overcomes something to how another person overcomes it can be very different. Like I stated earlier, it was around the seven-year mark that I finally accepted the way my life was. Throughout those seven years, there was anger, guilt, sadness, and self-pity. I would move in and out of the different stages, and many times I got stuck in some. When I would get stuck I remember praying. I would pray to God and ask for strength; I would ask for a lot more strength to get through this. I would talk with my mom and cry and say I could not go through this anymore. But I got through it. I got through it with faith and support.

There was no way on earth that I could have gotten through this loss alone. If I did not find my faith nor had I relied on my family and close friends for help and support, I would not be where I am today. I was broken from this injury. I was down emotionally from this injury. I could not recover from this injury on my own. Yes, there were the days when I would just want someone to pull the sheets over my head and leave me alone. I had those days, too. But what would save me was my mom coming in and saying, "Okay that's enough now, let's get going again." My mom would pick me back up again and again. My mom would let me stay down for only so long, then she would pick me up. Without her I may have just stayed down. I was and will always be so thankful for my parents love and support throughout my recovery.

Chapter Ten

Back to College

It was time now for me to go back to college. I had been out of the hospital for over a year and had been doing outpatient therapy from home. Three times a week, an occupational therapist would come to my parent's house and work with me on gaining more strength in my arms and more use of my hands. I was also having PT done at home to keep my leg muscles flexible so that when I did start walking again, they would be ready. Slowly, my body was getting stronger and stronger. However, my parents realized that I was doing nothing with my mind. So it was decided then that I should go back to school.

The campus that I was most familiar with was Kent State University. I had spent almost a full semester there before my accident, so I knew the layout pretty well. My parents and I had researched accessible campuses, and Kent State was one of the highest-ranked in Ohio for accessibility and services for students with a disability.

My other options for accessible campuses were Ohio State and Wright State. My sister had gone to Ohio State, and I remembered going to visit her when I was in high school. The campus was huge, and now that I was in a wheelchair, the big campus seemed even more overwhelming to me. Wright State was way too far away. (Wright State is close to Dayton, Ohio). So, since I had already gone to Kent State and was familiar with the campus, my parents and I decided that it would be the best fit for me to go back. Plus, Kent was only forty-five minutes from my parents' home and only about twenty-five minutes from my dad's insurance agency. With Kent being so close, I would be able to come home on the weekends and continue with my therapies.

Going back to school was a huge step and adjustment for both my parents and me. With me living at home up to that point, my mom had become my primary caregiver. What I mean by primary caregiver is that my mom was the one who helped me the most with my personal care: getting dressed, showering, going to the bathroom. I did have a woman that we hired through a nursing assistant agency helping me, but my mom was the main caregiver.

Every morning this woman would come to the house and help me get ready for my day. She would help me use the restroom, which consists of putting me on a bedpan while I was still in bed. I was very lucky to have gained the use of my bladder back, but the ability to hold it was weak. So as soon as this nurse's aide would get to the house, the first thing to do was get me on the bedpan because I would have to pee! From there, the aid would transfer me out of bed into my wheelchair, and we would be off to the shower to start the bathing process.

I would be transferred from my wheelchair to a shower chair that was mounted in the bathtub. Once I was secure on the shower chair, the aid would hand me my toothbrush and I would start out with brushing my teeth. Next, she would wash my hair and any other areas on my body that I was unable to reach. I was able to wash my upper body and my face pretty well.

From the shower it was back into my wheelchair, and then we would head back to my bedroom, where I would finish getting ready. In order to dress the lower part of my body, I would have to be put back into bed for the aid to put my pants on. Putting on pants meant rolling from side to side about ten times till the pants were securely up and in place. It is a good thing that I do not get motion sickness easily, because I would have to be taking Dramamine to get ready every morning. (I wonder if there is treatment for Dramamine addiction...hummm?) After getting my pants on, there would be one more final transfer back into my wheelchair, and then I would be ready for the day. Well, at least dressed for the day.

If for some reason the nurse's aides were unable to make it to get me up in the morning, my mom would be my backup. There were mornings when an aide would call off and the agency would be unable to send someone else out to the home. So my mom would have to get me dressed and up in my wheelchair before she would go off to work. On these mornings, I would have to bypass the shower and do a bed bath because it was quicker and easier on my mom. My mom was still working full-time as a nurse at Medina General Hospital, so having to get me up before work was a lot of work on her, but she always did it. Plus, my mom knew how much I loved the shower, so when she got home from work, she would put me in the shower and bathe me. I know for a fact that she was exhausted, but she would still do this for me. I will say it again, I was and will always be thankful for the most amazing mom in the world.

With me going back to college, my parents and I had decided it would be best if I lived on campus. I had lived on campus before, but this was a huge adjustment for all of us. At first, my mom and dad were both very reluctant for me to live on my own, considering how much care I needed. I will say that I was a little nervous as well.

Since the beginning of this whole life-changing event, my parents were always there. If I dropped something, one of them would pick it up. If I needed something I could not reach or get, one of them would get it for me. So for them, me moving out on my own meant huge worries and fears.

We discussed the possibility of me commuting to and from school, but when we looked at the cost of hiring someone to drive me to school, sit and wait for me while I was in class, and then drive back home, it was just going to cost way too much. So we set up an appointment with the Disabled Student Services Department at Kent State to start the ball rolling for me to get back to school. Life was now starting to get back to normal—a new and different normal.

My sister went with me to my appointment with Disabled Student Services. I met with the director of the department, and she thoroughly went over all the services that I was eligible for. She explained to me that I could have a note taker for my lecture classes. Also, I would be allotted more time for test taking and would be able to take my tests at the offices of Disabled Student Services instead of taking the test with the rest of the class in the classroom.

The director went over the transportation services available on campus for students with disabilities. She discussed with me and my sister what dorms were designated as residencies for a person in a wheelchair and told us that these dorms had cafeterias located in them. This was because I would not have to leave my dorm to eat. I already knew that my old dorm, Prentice Hall, was one of the dorms for disabled students because I remembered seeing the girls in wheelchairs when I lived there before. So I had already planned on going back to that dorm. I figured I knew Prentice Hall pretty well and where all the classroom buildings were located from that dorm.

I can say now, sending me back to college was the best *and* worst thing my parents could have ever done for me at that time in my life. I was not doing much of anything with my life at that point, except for therapies, which, of course, were very important at that time. But I was also falling into this rut of sitting at home, watching mind-rotting television, and waiting for my body to remember how it worked again. Therapy–good, mind rotting–not good.

So, with that being known, let me first cover why it was the worst thing they could have done. I was totally dependent on them! Hello?! Would a parent send a one-year-old baby off to a place where they would not be able to take care of themselves? No. Would a mother bird push a baby bird out of the nest if it could not fly? No. Well, I think not, but I have never asked a mother bird. But you see what I am getting at. I was all of these– a baby not able to fly and helpless, so to speak.

On the other hand, the best thing my parents could have done was put me back into college. I *needed* to learn how to be independent again. I was a twenty-two-year-old woman, and I needed to learn how to handle my new life and move forward. It was a change, though, and nobody, regardless of disability, cares a lot for change. Especially *big* change.

Sometimes people can get stuck in where they are in their life, particularly when a traumatic event happens to them. It is almost like life stops. A person may feel sorry for themselves and say, why me? Why are all these negative things happening to me? They may sit around waiting for something or someone to change how they feel or what is going on in their life. We want our old lives back. But, deep down inside, we know that is not going to happen.

I have learned that a person *should* feel this way and that all these feelings are normal. Unfortunately, trauma and negative things happen, and a person is left to relearn how to live again. In some situations like mine, where I put myself in harm's way and had to learn the hard way of the negative outcomes of destructive decision-making, I had to accept and learn to deal with these consequences. I did say, why me? And I felt sorry for myself. But the key was not getting stuck in these feelings.

I had to learn to pull myself out of these low, feeling sorry for myself, depressed feelings. Sometimes people believe that their external environment controls how they think or feel, so they may surround themselves with happy things and people that make them feel good. At that time, though, when I looked around me, I saw sadness, sadness for a body that did not work the way it used to work. I also saw familiarity. All around me was my hometown where I grew up. The roads I drove. I would see friends I went to school with, and they were walking. Seeing and remembering how I used to live my life was hard.

What I had to do to move on from these feelings was look ahead, which meant looking inward. I had to really look inside myself and find strength. And it was hard. I have learned through research that it is actually our internal world that controls us. People actually have the power to internally perceive how they want to live their life, whether they want to be happy or sad, living or not living, enjoying life and embracing it or letting it slip by. If we let ourselves believe that this is life now, looking around us and seeing everything negative, we will remain stuck in that place.

Luckily for me, my mom and dad knew that as hard as it was on them, I needed a nudge back into a new life. Well, actually, I needed more than a nudge. I needed to be physically picked up and put in the car and driven there, but now I am thankful my parents did this.

My mom had helped me hire and train the girls that would be helping me throughout the day at school. The disabled student services provided us with a list of students interested in providing attendant care to individuals with disabilities. Attendant care is just another name for nurse's aides or any other words people use for personal care. Once I got all my girls hired and lined up to help me with my daily care, this eased my mom's nerves a bit. She could then begin to see that this whole move towards independence was the best thing ever. For me, my new independent life was starting to take hold.

What are those cliché sayings that people say when things go awry? When it rains it pours, or when life hands you lemons, you should make lemonade. Yeah, those little sayings. Well, I have a new one to add to those: When your first week of college sucks, you should quit! I doubt that my first week of classes as a disabled student could have gone any worse.

Let me begin the horrible adventure. The week started off with me getting stuck in a pouring rainstorm the very first day of classes. I did not know that the belts that powered my wheelchair could not get wet, so when I ventured out to class and it was lightly drizzling, I thought, *no big deal. So what if I get a little wet?* What came out of nowhere, though, as I made my way further and further from my dorm down a hill to the building where my class was, was the hardest, quickest rainstorm I had ever seen in my life. As I turned my wheelchair around to head back to my dorm, the belts slipped off the motor of my chair, leaving me powerless to move. *I wanted to die.* I was sitting out in a pouring rainstorm, by myself, with no way to move. Just then, two (hot) guys came up behind me and asked if I needed help. I said yes without thinking, and they ended up pushing my power wheelchair uphill back to my dorm. The whole time I was sitting there saying over and over in my mind, *I cannot do this. I cannot be on my own. Screw independence!!*

As the guys pushed me into the lobby of my dorm, one of the girls that lived next to me was going out and asked if I was okay. She and I had become friends, and she knew that I was nervous about my first day of school. She must had noticed the look on my face, that I was about to cry, because she quickly thanked the guys for helping me and pushed me back to my dorm room. As soon as we got into my room, I burst into tears and said that I could not do this.

She ended up staying with me that morning, missing her first class that day, to sit with me and dry me off. She kept encouraging me that yes, I could do this, that this was just a little bump in the road. As she was saying all this I was thinking, *yeah, easy for you to say, you can walk to class or carry a flipp'n umbrella.* But she dried me off, put on my rain jacket, and we called the disabled student services transportation service and scheduled a ride for me to get to my next class. It was from that experience that I learned to use the disabled student transportation system when the weather did not look so good; I even used it if it was slightly cloudy out. I was not taking any chances.

The week was just getting started. After the rain adventure came the "stuck in the elevator ordeal," but luckily, it was not on the same day. The elevator ordeal happened a day or two later and was extremely scary. And, to boot, I did not have the two hot guys (making being stuck in the rain seem a little bit okay) to go through the elevator ordeal with me, either!

It all began with me having an evening class across campus. I had ventured out on my own since the skies looked clear, and I knew where the building was located. So I headed out to class and got to the building with no problems. This small venture had boosted my feeling of confidence and independence, and I remember that I had started to rethink my feelings that I could not do this college-by-myself thing. My spirits, at that time, were starting to look up.

My class was on the second floor of the building, and I had found the entrance with the handicap push plate, no problem. I pushed the handicapped blue plate, and open sesame, I was in the building. Not having to ask someone to open the door was a great feeling. I was experiencing independence. I quickly located the elevator and pressed the button to go up. I remember feeling yet another positive feeling of independence coming over me. I entered the elevator, and the doors had closed behind me. I looked from side-to-side to push the button. I saw the buttons, but I couldn't reach them. At first, I did not panic. I tried to maneuver my chair as much as I could to get closer to the button panel, but to no avail. It was at that point in time that I remember panic starting to set in.

Several minutes had gone by and all I could think of was, *My God, I have survived a car crash and broke my neck to now die in an elevator, by myself. No way is this happening!*

Remember me saying that my class was in the evening? Well, not as many people are in the building for an evening class compared to a day class, and it was a rarity that someone would use the elevator during the evening. I remember backing my chair into the door of the elevator several times and yelling for help. Nothing. Silence. Out of the corner of my eye, I could see the open door button. If I could just get to, I would be free. I remembered how many times I had pressed elevator buttons throughout my life, and now I really, really needed to, but could not. I was in total panic.

I was probably in there for twenty to twenty-five minutes before a professor used the elevator to take an overhead projector up to the second floor. I remember, when those elevator doors opened, I floored my wheelchair in reverse and came flying out of that elevator. I was never so thankful to be out of somewhere in my life, including the eight weeks of traction with weights hanging from my head, or my eleven-month stay in the rehabilitation hospital.

I believe I scared the "bajesus" out of that professor. Because, as much as I was relieved to be free of my incarceration in the elevator, I am pretty sure that when he went to press that elevator button that evening, he did not think a wild woman speeding backwards in a wheelchair screaming, "Dear Heavenly Father... Thank you, thank you!" was going to be coming out of the doors. The lesson I took away from that ordeal was from then on I would back my wheelchair into elevators and quickly take notice of where the buttons were located inside the door. Even to this day, if the buttons look to be out of reach, I quickly zoom forward in my wheelchair and find someone to help me with the elevator. What's the old saying? Once bitten, twice shy? In my case, once trapped in an elevator, twice ain't gone happen. Or something like that.

But that was it. I was done. Done with being in school. Done with trying to be independent. I was done with this new, different life. First getting stuck in the rain, now the elevator. Nope. I was going home. I was thinking and saying to myself at that point that I was going to live the rest of my life with my parents, raise cats, and paint pictures with my mouth. At that time my thoughts were that this whole college thing was way too scary and unknown, and that there was no way I was going to be able to handle it. My external world had won. At that time, I was not even handling being in a wheelchair well, let alone being in a wheelchair on my own in college. I was just done.

I called my mom and dad when I got back to my dorm that night crying hysterically that did not want to be there and that they needed to come get me right then. My mom listened to me tell her what had happened: the rain, being soaking wet in front of two of the hottest guys on campus, the elevator trauma. She listened and let me cry.

When I had managed to calm down and had stopped crying, she assured me that things would get better and that I needed to give it more time. *More time!? What? You are not coming to get me? Did she not just hear what I had been through in the first week of classes? Was I talking to some kind of Robot Mom? How dare they not love and want to protect me! Do my parents not understand how incredibly hard it was to be in this damn wheelchair and try to function, day after day?*

I found out later that my mom's first thought and motherly instinct, as I was telling her about these horrible things happening to her baby, was to get in the car and come get me right then and there. She wanted to bring me home, and we would just figure something else out. She told me that, as I was hysterically telling her what had happened to me, she too was crying. But she knew in her heart that coming to get me, rescuing me, or shielding me from bad, unexpected things happening to me, would be the worst thing she could do. Me, being on my own in school, was the best thing for me. But of course, I did not understand *any* of that at all because I was not a parent.

What *I* understood was that my parents did not care about me, and I was on my own.

My mom later shared with me that this particular experience was the hardest thing for her and my dad. For her to sit back and leave me at school and see me hit obstacle after obstacle and not come running to fix everything was incredibly hard. My parents knew that as much as I needed to learn how to feed myself again in the early stages of this injury, I also needed to learn to live again without them.

I really learned a lot about myself re-entering life after this injury. I found that I had an inner strength that I had no idea was in me. Up until my injury and throughout the early stages of recovery, I always felt like I was a pretty strong and confident person. Before the car crash, I dealt with obstacles or challenges in my life pretty well.

However, after the car crash, dealing with this injury was a lot of ups and downs of emotions. I found that I relied on more of an inner strength, more so than my outer appearance to get through the obstacles and challenges that my new life had. I had thought I was a strong person, but I was now experiencing my true strength.

And I never had a problem with confidence. I was always fairly confident with myself. Regardless of whether it was sports, cheerleading, dating, whatever, that is one area that I did not lack. And if I did feel less confident, I would not show it outwardly. I think the saying goes–fake it 'til you make it.

Things were different now. When it came to overcoming the thousands of changes that my life had to make in order to move forward with this injury, I teetered from strong to weak. My confidence was up and strong as long as I had my parents around me. My parents were my safety net. Again, this goes back to me saying that a strong support network around a person when they are going through major life-changing events or consequences is key to that person achieving success. Whenever I felt like there was no way I could go through *all* these changes, my parents would pick me back up. If a change was relatively small, I was okay. But there are few relatively small changes with an injury like mine. My family and friends would tell me that I could do this, that I could overcome this injury, but could I? I would hear their words, and I could see the encouraging looks on their faces, but did I feel strong enough to do it? *Was I strong enough to do this?*

So basically, I never really had to or tried to access anything deep within myself to get something or go somewhere in life. Not until after this car crash. It was then that I had to find strength to stand up again. Not on my two feet, so-to-speak, but stand up for myself. I'm not going to lie; this was the hardest challenge ever in my life. Finding my inner strength was hard. Having to adapt to the way my life was now was overwhelming. But life does go on, and even the least likely person that you can think of can handle challenges.

Now if I needed help, I had to learn to ask for it. If I dropped something, I had to ask someone to pick it up. If I had to go to the bathroom, I had to ask someone to help me go. The little things that just about everyone takes for granted in their lives were gone from me, and I now had to ask for help to do these tasks. Of course I could deny that I needed help. I never had to ask for help before. But what was I trying to prove? If I dropped a book, I needed to pick it up. If I needed to pee, well... you all know what would be next. Bottom line though, was it was hard to accept that I needed help and that this was the way my life was now.

Before I went off to college, my parents were my main source for helping me. If I needed help doing something or if I was struggling in some way, my parents were right there.

My parents were not strangers. They were people who understood my limitations and needs. They did not have pity for me or worse yet, feel sorry for me. One of my biggest obstacles being back at school was now having to ask a total stranger to help me. That was hard to do.

I did not want someone to feel sorry for me or pity me. I did not want to be looked at as a different or lesser person, so to speak. So I would just not ask. I would just wing it or go without until someone who I knew, a safe person, would come along. I would ask him or her to help me. Well, that thought would be all good if I lived in fairytale land where politicians did not lie and the check was really in the mail. But realistically, I would eventually have to ask a stranger for assistance.

What I came to find out over time was that it was more me putting these thoughts or feelings of sorry-ness on myself, not the people helping me. For the most part, I truly believe that people, when asked by someone for help, do not even think much about it. They help the person and move on. What I was doing at that time, though, was putting these irrational beliefs in my head that these people felt sorry for me, and that they were thinking, "Thank God I am not like this girl." Okay, they still might have been saying, "Thank God I'm not like this girl," but the thought had nothing to do with my disability.

What I came to see was that I was my own worst enemy and a self-sabotager (it is a word in my world) at that time in my recovery. Because apparently, not only could I not walk, but now I could read the minds of the people that were around me.

I eventually moved on from feeling this way due to several factors. The main and only real factor was that my friends that I had met after my crash never thought of me any differently than any of their other friends. I was just their friend, Barb... Who happened to be in a wheelchair. They basically knew me no other way than as wheelchair

Barb, or, as one of my dearest friends would call me, "Wheelchair Girl." Which was okay, because he was "Wheelchair Boy." And, boy, did I ever become super popular around Christmas time. Now it took me a while to figure out why I had so many friends at this time of year, and I couldn't figure out why these new friends wanted to go shopping all the time. But then it hit me. They got to park close at the mall! Yep. That was it. Even to this day, when I drive (yes, I drive) and pull in to park, my friend's immediate reactions are, "That's right, we get to park close, legally."

I ended up meeting some of my best friends in the world when I went back to school after my injury, and little did I know, the man that I would marry.

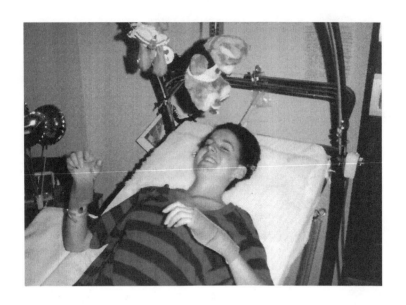

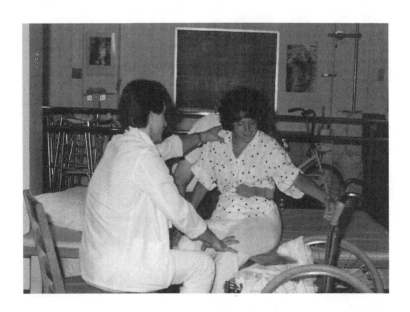

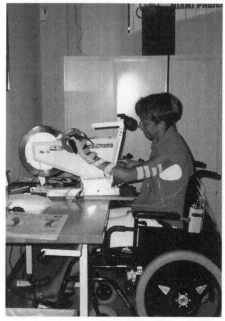

Barb Frye

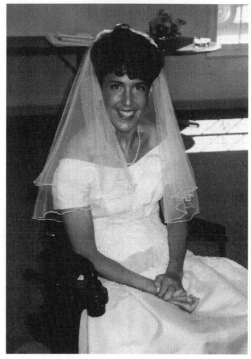

Barb Frye

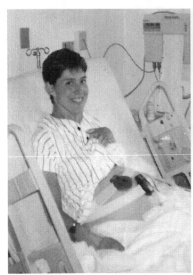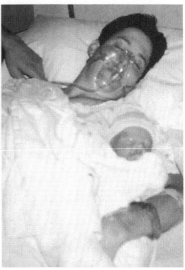

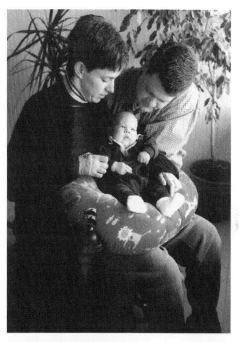

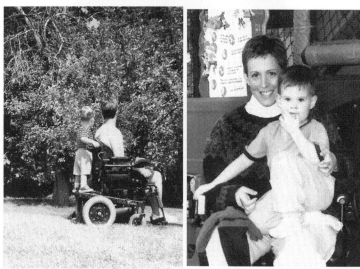

Barb Frye

Chapter Eleven
Normal Things

Things were going well. I was back in college, getting to my classes on my own, and managing my attendant care. Life was starting to move forward. I was starting to do a lot of the normal things that I did before my injury: going out with friends, living on my own. But the one thing I was *not* thinking about getting back to was dating. Dating was not something that was even on my radar. I had dated before my injury, but I was pretty much set to not going back to that normal thing for a very long time, if ever.

To me, dating meant closeness, touch, feeling, and being together with someone, alone. Dating meant movement, holding hands, or hugging. All the things that I remember doing when I dated but now could not do. Therefore, I was not going to go there. Not as a disabled person. I had just decided the best thing for me to do was get through college, live with my parents forever, and raise cats (I love cats, and dogs, too). And I was fine with that.

Basically, I did not want any guy to know that my body was different. Not different looking by any means; I still had two boobs, and they were still located on my chest, and my lady parts where still located down south. But my body felt different; it did not move like normal bodies move.

In my case, my sensation from the breastbone up was normal. But from the breastbone down, it started to decrease. And there was no rhyme or reason to my sensation. Some areas of my body had close to normal feeling in it, while other areas were not so normal. If you were to touch or pinch me in certain areas, nothing. I would have no clue you were doing anything to me. By the way, this is considered normal recovery of sensation in an incomplete spinal cord injured person. Finally I was fitting into a normal category, as far as recovery from a spinal cord injury goes, that is.

One question that I am often asked today when I am making speaking presentations is, what is it like to be paralyzed? The best comparison I have come up with in my situation. You know when a body part falls asleep? It feels real thick, numb, and tingly? That is how my body feels for the most part from the chest down.

So, knowing before my injury what dating entailed, I was just not going to do it. However, my mind still thought *about* dating; I thought about what it would be like to be close to someone again—to be touched, to feel, and to be intimate. But there was no way. When my mind would wander to those thoughts, I would remind myself that the whole dating thing was just way too overwhelming, and I would be fine alone—with my cats, of course.

Well, so much for the not dating thing. Several of my girlfriends that I lived with in the dorm found out one day that I liked this guy that was one of the driver's of the van service that was available for students with disabilities at Kent State. And that was all it took. Word got back to him that I liked him, and before I knew it, I was agreeing to go to dinner with him. I remember thinking, *what in the 'H' did I just agree to do?*

I will never forget getting ready for that date as long as I live. I was a nervous damn wreck. If I could have gotten up out of my wheelchair and ran out of that dorm that night, I would have because I did so not want to go on that date. Not because I did not like this guy. Oh, I liked him; I was just "throw-up nervous." But since my running days were long gone, I had to buck-up, face the music, and go on this date. Plus, there was no way my friends were going to let me get out of it!

Actually, all my nervousness was for nothing. The date turned out great! We went to dinner and had a wonderful time. He did really well getting me in and out of the car. At that time in my recovery, I was using a transfer board to slide over from my wheelchair to the passenger seat of the car. My best friend, Debbie, showed him how to get me into the car with the transfer board, and I used my lightweight manual wheelchair that could be folded up and put into the trunk of his car. After dinner, we came back to the dorm, where of course all of my friends where waiting for me to get home, like nervous parents. Both my date and I thought that was quite funny. My date gave me a slight kiss on the cheek and said that he had a great time and that he would see me the next week during school.

We never went out again, which was fine, because we still remained good friends. I went out a few more times with other guys that I had met, but nothing really serious. I think I held back being serious with anyone because serious meant touch, and touch meant intimacy, and intimacy meant that the guy would know all about how my body was, and I was not ready for that. So going out with guys as good friends was just fine with me.

Then there was this one. A guy that managed to *weasel* his way past my insecure body issues, past my worrying about what my body would do or how my body would respond to touch, and got to me.

We started out as friends. Isn't that how it always starts out? He also worked for the disabled student transportation service (I must have a soft spot for a guy that wears a uniform and drives a modified transportation van!). I always thought that this guy was not bad looking, but he was my friend, Don, the van driver. There were no romantic thoughts there, or so I thought. But then one day, I kind of looked at him and thought, *you know, he's not bad looking. He's funny as heck. And he knows how to lock a wheelchair down in a van. Bonus!* So I thought, *what the heck, I would go out with him.* But he never asked me out. He would come over to my apartment to watch television. We would sit in the dark watching television, alone, and then he would leave.

He would come over, hang out, watch television, and that seemed to be the only thing we would do. To me, it seemed like he was only interested in being friends. So I just figured, oh well, we will just be friends, and that is fine. Then one day during finals week, he called me and asked if I wanted to go for a drive and just get away from campus for a while. I remember thinking for a minute that I probably should not go because I had so much studying to do. But I also knew that I kind of liked him, and he made me laugh. So I ended up going.

Well, there's no reason to say anymore. We started dating from that ride on. He ended up asking me if he could kiss me on the way home from the ride, and we have been together ever since. Donald (as I call him and as most of my family calls him as well) and I dated from August of '91 to August of '97. We got married on August 23, 1997. People will ask me, why did you guys date for so long? And I say, for several reasons, one being that Donald had to know all about my care and how my body worked and did not work. Nothing could be left unknown, as far as my care went. Donald had to realize that this was not going to get better.

I wanted Donald to know about my personal care. Yes, I had my attendants that helped take care of me *most* of the time. But Donald had to know my care as well. I had bladder and bowel care. I had to have my hair blown dry and styled. I had to have help getting dressed, stuff that the typical boyfriend does not do for his girlfriend when they are dating. Therefore, we dated for a long time.

Donald and I traveled together so that he could experience what it was like to get me up in the morning. He would have to help me in the shower, help me get dressed, help me go to the bathroom. He basically had to know *everything*. Even... sex. Let's face it, sex is a big part of a relationship, and if things are not compatible with both partners, the relationship may not be so good. Therefore, this had to be known.

Now, without getting *too* personal, sex was still doable. What do I mean by "sex was still doable"? I was still able to have sex. Was I able to feel sex? Yes. Did it feel like what sex felt like before my injury? No. But I could still feel something. If I remember correctly from my seventh grade health class, where I was first educated about sexual intercourse, I am using the proper terminology that my health teacher used back then, which made me and my friends giggle whenever he said it! And, by the way, I am *still* giggling. But I remember learning that the "lady-parts" area on a girl have lots of nerve endings, and when sex is occurring, those nerve endings get even more heightened. So, since my nerves from the chest line down where affected by the spinal injury, my lady-part nerves were affected as well. Luckily, though, I did regain sensation throughout my body, my lady-parts area being one of those areas, and am able to feel somewhat. Now, does it feel normal? (There is that *normal* word again!) No. But it does still feel pretty good. So much for not getting too personal. How's that for too much personal information?

We got married on August 23, 1997 and honeymooned in Martha's Vineyard. When we got back from our honeymoon, we lived where we had already been living, in a house that I had purchased before we got married. It was then that we started our married life together.

In 1996, Donald and I had found this little house that was the perfect starter house. It was an older ranch with a walkout basement. It needed minimal modifications for me to be able to live in it. Basically, the bathrooms needed to be ripped out and a modified shower stall needed to be put in. (This is my interpretation of minimal.)

The home had three bedrooms, one and a half baths, and a two-sided wood-burning fireplace that I loved. You could access the fireplace from both the living room and the dining room/kitchen area. It was the biggest fireplace

I had ever seen in my life. The awesome thing about the fireplace was that it was up off the floor by about two feet or so, so I could pull right up in front of the fireplace in my wheelchair. That meant that I could literally bake myself. Well, not literally bake myself, but as I've explained before, most spinal cord injured persons are known to be cold most of the time. I could be cold in July. No joke!

So, that being known, I would pull up right alongside that fireplace, and it was instant heaven. One thing that I had to be careful about, though, was that I did not get too close, where I could get burned. I was able to feel the heat of the fire on my face and all, but I would forget sometimes that my legs were even *closer* to the opening. Since the hot/cold sensations in my legs were not there anymore, I was at risk of getting burned. Donald would always feel the side of my leg that was closest to the fire and check if it was getting to hot. So, if my leg felt hot to his touch, I would back away from the fire some.

We lived there for seven years. Donald did all of the modifications to the house so I could function and move around in my wheelchair. He and several of our friends and family members built a ramp to the front door so I could get inside. Once I was inside, the house had a nice open floor plan. I had no problems getting around.

Besides our decorating touches to the house that made it adorable, the yard and landscaping were completely redone. One of my passions, come to find out, is gardening and landscaping. These are two great things if you are an able-bodied person. Not so great passions to have if you are a quadriplegic with limited hand use. But that did not stop me or Donald. We would go to the local greenhouse and buy plants and bushes, bring them home, and Donald would do the planting. After a few summers, our yard was beautiful.

Life was starting to move forward. I was married, living in a house that was *mine*, and driving. Oh yeah, driving. I forgot to mention that I had learned how to drive again. Let me back up a bit. In 1995, I started the process to learn to drive... And what a process it was.

I had only been driving for two years when the car crash happened. That being said, I wasn't necessarily the worst driver, but I certainly was not the best. (I'm sure my mom will be laughing when she reads this.) So, for two years, I drove a car normally. Both hands on the wheel, at ten o'clock and two o'clock and right foot used to brake and accelerator. At sixteen, I got my license on my first try, and I was off and driving. Piece-o-cake, basically.

Jump forward two years to when I was eighteen years old, paralyzed from the chest down, never to drive again (normally, that is) for the rest of my life. Thinking back on my before-crash driving experiences, little did I know the night of the car crash would be the last time I would drive my car again. That would be the last time I ever got out of a car from the driver's side door. (Isn't *that* weird!?) Come to think of it, it was the last time I would ever turn the key to start the car or put the car in gear using the shifter. In a second, I stopped doing those things the way I had done them for two years.

I did not pursue driving again until 1994. Up until that time, I really did not feel the need to relearn. That and, I do not think my parents were really excited about me learning to drive again. It was one thing for them to let go when I was sixteen and get my driver's license, but now I was in my twenties and disabled. Let's just say they did not push for my independence in the driving area as much as they pushed for me to be able to feed myself again. But I took the leap into learning to drive again, and my parents learned to accept my independence. Well, kind of accept it. To this day my mom *still* freaks out when I leave Medina County.

Learning to drive was just another step towards doing the normal thing that I had done before. And like all the other *normal* things that I had learned how to do again, learning to drive involved the inevitable hurdles of this injury that I needed to get over.

I started the process at Metro Health Center's driving school here in Cleveland. The first step in this adventure towards independence would be a series of tests to make sure I had the strength, reaction time, and basic ability to handle driving. The testing only took a couple of hours, and it was basically done on a driving simulator machine.

Since I would not be driving anymore with my feet, the test focused all on my arms and upper body strength. They had to test the strength in my arms to see if I would be able to pull back on the brake to stop the vehicle (which, of course, is a good thing to be able to do).

My brake and accelerator were now going to be located on the driver door and would be a throttle-type device with a tri-pin holder that my wrist slipped down into. I would push forward to accelerate and pull back to brake. This movement required that I have good strength in my shoulder, bicep, and wrist. I had no problems with that test.

As far as my reflex time, all was good too. During the testing, I would have to push a simulated accelerator, and when I saw a light flash, I would have to quickly stop accelerating and push another button. This test was done on me to see that my reflexes and reaction time were quick enough to react in an emergency situation. Again, I did not have any problems with this test. So, with two major tests done and both passed with flying colors, it was then determined that I was ready to actually get into the modified van that Metro used to test individuals out on the road. Basically, I had to do so many test runs, or parking lot hours as I called them, before it was determined that I was road-ready.

For the next several weeks, I would be driven up to Metro's east side campus where their adaptive driving program was located and spend about two to three hours a session driving around the many parking lots of the hospital's campus. We spent several sessions on accelerating and stopping, making left turns and right turns. Then we would advance to making left turns that were going downhill and right turns going uphill or vice versa. I was amazed at how much time we spent on turning and stopping and doing these tasks. I was quickly made aware of how much strength and upper body use that these movements took. I had never thought of the muscle groups that I was using when I learned to drive before. Truthfully, I doubt many people really ever think about all the muscle they use when driving. But when a person loses the use of those muscles and has to struggle and work hard to get them back, they become aware of the role those muscles played in the everyday act of driving a car.

Not only did my awareness of the strength I needed in my arms to drive become known, but it was also quickly brought to my attention how much abdominal and back muscles we use to drive. For example, having me drive down hill and turn left halfway down showed my driving instructor that I needed lateral supports on my chair to help me stay upright when turning. This way, when I turned, I could rely on the lat supports to stabilize my trunk so I did not fall over in my chair. Frankly, falling over your chair while turning, or falling in your chair anytime while driving, is frowned upon by the instructor. Go figure.

I had six months of driver's ed for about three to four hours a day, two days a week. I did not mind these required hours because I wanted to make sure that I had the strength and ability to drive a vehicle. My instructor and I would spend hour after hour driving around the campus of Metro Hospital, making left turns, then right turns. We would do moving turns to the right and moving turns to the left, and each time my instructor would have me increase my speed to simulate what it would be like out on the open roads. As my speeds increased, it was determined that I would also need a chest strap to help support my upper body. Basically, this chest strap was an airport-type seat belt that would be attached to my chair, and when I was driving I could buckle the seat belt across my chest. This gave me more restraint in my upper body so that if I needed to slam the brakes, I would not be flung forward from the waist up.

We found out the hard way that I needed this chest strap when I was going down a slight incline on the hospital campus. As my driving instructor asked me to stop the van, I pulled back on my brake lever to stop and could not get the van to stop without falling forward. We went through an intersection and came to an abrupt stop up on a curb. Thank God it was an intersection in the parking lot of the hospital and not a busy intersection out on the road. By the time it came for me to venture out on the open road, I looked like a Formula One race car driver with a four-point harness and crash helmet. Okay, that may be a slight exaggeration, but it is not too far off.

Oh, the open road–wind whipping through my hair, radio jamming out to George Thorogood's "Bad to the Bone." All right, not exactly, but my window *was* down and my hair *was* being blown around.

The roads my instructor first took me out on were residential, thirty-five-mile-per-hour roads. To most drivers, thirty-five miles per hour spells frustration and slow moving. To me, though, thirty-five miles per hour seemed like I was moving at the speed of light.

I remember one time my driving instructor telling me to pull over on the side of the road at the next chance I had. I remember thinking to myself, *I wonder if he's going to get sick or what?* It turned out he was having me pull off to let the stream of cars that had built up behind me go by. I guess it looked like a parade forming behind this huge Metro driving van or a funeral procession going down the road, minus the flags.

One of the momentous days that I will never forget is when I finally drove forty-five miles per hour. Of course, today, I am not proud, or maybe I am proud, to say that I got my first speeding ticket coming home from Chicago on the Ohio turnpike. Eighty in a sixty-five! Pretty impressive, huh? I had come a long way from being a nervous thirty-five-miles-per-hour driver to an eighty-miles-per-hour driver.

In the end, it took me three tries to get my driver's license. Not because I couldn't drive well, but I think the driving instructors who rode with me and administer the driving test were not really comfortable evaluating a person with my type of disability. I was required to take my driving test down in Columbus, Ohio because I had to use the modified van that Ohio State Driving School uses for evaluating potential drivers with limitations.

The first try at my license was a complete disaster. The tie-down that held my wheelchair in place behind the steering wheel came loose during a left turn. When I made the turn, my chair shifted, causing me to pull back on the accelerator. The driving instructor failed me for doing forty-five in a twenty-five. When I slowed down to explain to her that my chair was not secure in the lock down and that it caused me to pull back on the accelerator, she wanted to hear nothing about it and instructed me to drive back to the test station. When we arrived back to the test center, my instructor came out, fully expecting and excited to hear the news that I passed. The bad news was abruptly clarified by the state driving instructor as she jumped out of the van before I even came to a complete stop and informed him that I failed because I *could not* control the van.

Second time's a charm, right? Wrong. My instructor and I figured we would try the other side of town for this test. It turned out that Columbus's south side DMV testing center was tougher. The second time I took the test, which was a week after my first attempt, the instructor failed me before I even got out of the parking lot.

This test started out just fine. My instructor made sure my chair was tried down securely to assure no problems like the first attempt. The DMV instructor got into the van and instructed me to drive out of the parking lot and turn left onto the roadway. While I was exiting the parking lot before I go any further let me set the scene here. When leaving a parking lot, there are designated lanes, which are necessary to follow while exiting onto the road which lead to the main thoroughfare, which in turn leads out to the road. Of course, most people will just cut across parking lots to get to the exit quickly. But, since I was taking my driver's test and cutting across the parking lot is an automatic fail, I followed *all* of the rules and requirements for exiting a parking lot properly.

I proceeded to back out of the parking space and head down the row to the main thoroughfare. From there, I was instructed to head to the traffic light and make a left onto the main road. No problem. Simple pimple.

As I was heading down the parking lot row, a car came out of nowhere, cutting me off and causing me to brake suddenly. Up until this point, the test instructor had been looking down, writing stuff on a note pad, not really paying attention to what was going on. When I braked quickly, he looked up and saw the car right in front of us. He asked me if I saw that car in front of me and asked why I was so close to it. I responded that the car must have come cutting across the parking lot and out of nowhere, cut me off.

I remember that he looked at me, looked at the car in front of me, looked back at the open parking lot, and then asked me to circle the van around back to the building. I did what he asked, and as I came to a stop in front of the driver's bureau, *my* instructor came out of the driving center, inquiring as to why we came back to the building. The test instructor said that he did not feel that I had good control of the vehicle and that I cut a car off in the parking lot.

Well, without going into *great* detail, let's just say my driving instructor *strongly* disagreed with this instructor. It turned out that he was watching the whole time from the building and saw the car cutting across the parking lot. But the instructor administering the test always wins. I had to come back to Columbus a third time to conquer the driver's license hurdle!

So it's *third time's* a charm, not second. I got it. And I also got my driver's licenses after the third try. Whoooohoooo! There was *no way* I was coming back for a fourth try, believe you me. No siree. I was done with

Columbus driving test people and done making the trip down to Columbus to try yet *another* DMV to see if those test people were more comfortable testing a driver with a disability. I passed the test, got my license, and I got back home. Now it was just a matter of getting my own van modified so I could drive it myself.

I purchased my first vehicle ever in October of 1995. It was a '95 Ford Econoline E-150 van, a deep cherry wine color, and she was all mine. I did not get to drive the van until the following year in April because it was shipped down to a van modifier in Columbus. (What is it with me, Columbus, and driving?) They had the van for roughly six months so they could install all the equipment I needed to drive.

I remember the day we went to pick up the van. It was late April, and it was actually a nice spring day, a rarity in Ohio. Donald, my dear friend Barb, and myself headed down to Columbus to bring *my* van home. We got down to Columbus mid-afternoon and went over all the modifications that had been done to the van by the modifier. They had cut into the floor of my van and lowered it ten inches. This was done to give my head clearance, since I would be driving right from my wheelchair. They installed an automatic lock-down system in the driver's seat area. This device allowed me to roll in behind the steering wheel, and the locking system would sense my wheelchair and automatically lock my chair in place.

I had a console of toggle switches located between the passenger seat and me that allowed me to put my windows up or down, turn my lights on, and tune my radio. Basically, everything that would be located on the dashboard of a car was placed on this console with a switch that I would be able to work.

When I hit a switch, a headrest would swing in behind my head once I was in place behind the wheel. The headrest had buttons on it for the horn, my bright light, and my turn signals. If I would be driving down the road and someone pulled out in front of me, I could push my head back into the headrest, hitting my horn. I think the headrest was missing a devise so that when I hit the button for the horn, not only would the horn sound, but also a cardboard cutout of a hand with just the middle finger sticking up would pop-up. What? Am I not entitled to let the jacka** who pulled out in front of me know that I think he is number one?

I drove my new van around the parking lot before I ventured out onto the street. There were lots of adjustments to make to the controls that were put into the van before I was road-ready. Once all the adjustments were done and everything was tweaked to me, I remember taking *her* out onto the road. My heart was racing. This was *my* van and I was driving it for the first time. It was one of the coolest feelings ever!

I could not believe it was happening. My steps towards being more independent really took a ginormous leap forward. One thing I remember thinking as I was driving my van at that time was a memory from when I was back at Parma Hospital. When I was newly injured, my social worker would say things to me like, *this will get easier, and you will do things that you once did before.* And guess what? I was. I was driving again. It just took me ten years and five months to do it, but hey, I was driving!

Donald ended up driving my van home from Columbus that day because I was not real comfortable driving on the highways. To be honest, and I know several of my friends reading this book will attest to this confession, it took me *years* to go over forty-five miles per hour when I was driving. Yes, I know what you are asking: How do you get a speeding ticket for doing eighty then? Let me just say that over the last several years, I have developed a bit of a *lead arm.*

Besides not being comfortable driving fast, I was also not comfortable driving on the highways. For many years, I would take the back roads to wherever I needed to go. I knew every back road to *every* mall within forty miles of my parent's house. Granted, it would take me twice as long to *get* to the mall, but I was at least driving there myself. Being able to drive somewhere, *by myself, when I wanted to*, was worth every *out-of-the-way* time increase to get there.

Over time, I got comfortable driving on the highways, and once that comfort came, the open road was mine! I would become comfortable driving everywhere. When we went on family trips, I would drive. Virginia, Maryland, wherever we would go, I would drive. If I were to get tired or just did not feel like driving anymore, my van was adapted so that my husband or any other able-bodied person who was traveling with me could drive. But it was very seldom that I did not want to drive.

Chapter Twelve

I'm What?

I suppose when a woman hears that she is pregnant there can be several different responses and reactions. For instance, there are responses like, *"Oh my Gosh, that is great!"* or *"Oh my Gosh, are you kidding me?"* And then there are the feelings that go along with hearing that you are pregnant: excitement, joy, or being pissed. Yes, pissed.

Well, "I'm What?" was the thought racing through my head as well as the words coming out of my mouth when my doctor told me over the phone that I was five weeks pregnant. I remember saying, "Seriously... Are you sure? How?" And my doctor's response was, "Yes, yes, and I think you know how." (At least he is a lady parts doctor with a sense of humor!)

See, prior to this phone conversation happening, my doctor and I had had several conversations regarding my ability to conceive a baby. He had told me all along that since my menstrual cycle was regular there should not be an issue with me being able to conceive. Of course, he went on to explain that there were no guarantees to a woman being able to conceive, disability or no disability.

We also talked about the what ifs. What if I could not conceive naturally? He explained that if I could not conceive naturally, then we could look into fertility. That's easy enough; I remember thinking, *fertility it will probably be.*

I came out of that doctor's appointment that day thinking, or should I say assuming, that in order for me to conceive, we would have to do fertility. Why did I think this from what he and I had discussed? Well, because conceiving naturally would be too normal-like. And up until that point in this whole recovery and acceptance of this injury, nothing had been normal. Therefore, why should conceiving a baby be different? Also, Don and I had been having an intimate relationship for several years, and we never had a close call or even thought at any point that I might be pregnant. Yes, we were using preventative measures most of the time, but there were several, let's say, heated occasions when prevention was overlooked.

And I do not care how careful the guy says or thinks he can be, or how in control he says he is on the releasing of his swimmers. There is something called a scout swimmer. Or if I have to use the proper medical terminology, I will: pre-ejaculation. I personally think that scout swimmer is a funner word, though. And yes, funner is a word, too.

Here's a funny story. My husband is Catholic. For those Catholics out there reading, you will get a chuckle out of this. One time when my husband and I were in a heated moment, we did not have any protection with us. So my husband says, "That's okay, I will just pull and pray." Now, I was raised Protestant, and I had never heard of this technique before. So I assumed (there is that bite-you-in-the bum word again) that this must be a *Catholic thing,* so I just went along with it. In my world, Catholic beliefs trump Protestants', so I went with the bigger belief following (joke).

Here's an educational tip for Catholic boys: Pull-n-Pray is not an effective birth control method. Just putting that disclaimer out there. Sometime in November of 1997, my husband did not pray *hard* enough, and we conceived a baby normally.

My Doc: You are five weeks pregnant.

Me: What?

My Doc: You are pregnant.

Me: Seriously?

My Doc: Yes.

Me: How? We did not go to Metro Hospital. I thought you said fertility.

I remember sitting there at my desk at work that day. I had just hung up the phone with my doctor and was thinking to myself, *oh-my-gosh, I'm pregnant! I am pregnant!* To say that every single thing went through my head at that time would be an understatement because *more* than everything went running through my head.

I was pregnant. I was pregnant with a baby that would need to be fed, bathed, changed, dressed, taken care of, rocked, and held. When I looked at the things that this baby would need done, several of those things on that list were things that *I* needed done for *me* with this injury. I remember feeling two distinct feelings at that time: excitement and terror. Excitement, because all my young life, what I wanted more than anything was to be a mom. Terror, because how was I going to take care of this baby when *I* needed to be taken care of?

As a young girl growing up, I wanted to be a mom. I remember playing house when I was young, and my stuffed animals or cat would play my child. I would dress my child, bath them (Snickers, my cat, was not real *keen* on the bathing, for that matter, the dressing either), and feed them—basically, I tried to do everything a mom does when she has a child. I would think to myself that someday I would get married, have two-point-seven kids, and be the best, most caring mom there ever was.

Side note: What is it with the point-whatever child? Two-point-five kids, two-point-seven kids? It's that third child that gets stuck with the point-five-or-seven number. He's a child, right? So isn't he justified in receiving the full value of one whole? Does this child not mean as much as the first two? Or do you just not *give-it-your-all* when it comes down to conceiving the third child?

My intense curiosity about this point-seven child thing may stem to the fact that I am the third child. Therefore, did I not receive as much nurturing from my parents? Did they not set as much aside for college for their point-seven child because chances were that they weren't going to be college material?

Obviously, I am joking here. But since I am on the subject of the number of children to have, if you are thinking about how many children you want to have, think about the psychological damage you could be causing your third child if you choose to have three. See, like I said, I am the third child.

When we would go places as a family, let's say dinner, there were *always* tables for four open. We would have to wait for a big table to open up because we where a party of five. I could see my siblings eyes as they looked over at me while we would wait for the bigger table to come available, and I knew they were thinking, *only if mom and dad would have just stopped a two, we would be eating by now.* Psychological damage, I tell you! Or, if we would go to an amusement park, my mom and dad would be paired together, my sister and brother would be together, and then there was me, all alone. And guess what? That meant I would either have to sit out the ride or better yet, have to ride with stranger danger.

What's the message behind my rant? Have two children, four children, or six children. Okay, if you have six children, there is something seriously wrong with you or you are mega rich. *Another* very important thing to keep in mind as you are contemplating having kids or how many to have: never let the children outnumber the parents–anarchy may occur. Don't say you were not warned.

Okay, back to finding out that I was pregnant. I could not believe what my doctor had just told me. I was five weeks pregnant? How was I going to tell Don? Yes, we planned on having children, but I think we both thought that we would have to *really* plan, giving us time to discuss having a child. And now I was sitting at my desk thinking that we did not plan for this to happen, and what the heck are we going to do? I also remember thinking, *what if Don is not happy about it?* Or, *what if he thinks that this was not a good time? We have only been married four-ish months, and what if Don wanted to wait longer to start our family?* Needless to say, I was excited, scared, overwhelmed, and really, really nervous as to how I was going to tell Don the news.

In order to give me more time to process the news, I ended up waiting a couple days to tell him. Don had known that I was going to my doctor for a check up to see why I was not feeling good, but I truly believe he thought I just had the flu or something female-related. You know how men can be when they hear the words "female issues." The less they know, the better they feel. I do not think, or let me rephrase that, I know that he did not think that I could be pregnant. He prayed, for God's sake!

On the day I told him, we had been shopping the after-Christmas sales at the mall. We had spent a good three hours walking around the mall, and I could not find a good opportunity to tell him. We left the mall and Don was driving my modified van. As we were getting on the highway heading home, for some reason, the mood to tell him struck me. I remember Don turning onto the entrance ramp to get on the highway and starting to accelerate to merge into traffic. I could see his face in the rearview mirror, and for some reason, I thought this was the best time ever to tell him the exciting news.

I asked him if he remembered me telling him that I had gone to the doctor regarding me not feeling good. He had remembered. I then said to him that the doctor had called me, and I knew now why I had not been feeling good. The whole time we are having this conversation, I can see his face and facial expressions in the rearview mirror, and keep in mind, at this time, he is merging into traffic.

I went on telling him that the doctor had ran blood work on me, and the blood work had come back with a conclusive answer as to why I was not feeling well. I remember him nodding, and I went on to say that it turned out that I was five weeks pregnant. He looked at me in the mirror and stared at me for what seemed like a long time. He asked me something like, are you serious? I responded with yes and reminded him to look back at the road, because traffic was kind of heavy. We rode in silence for several minutes, and then I remember him looking at me in the mirror and smiling.

For the rest of the drive home, we talked about if we were ready for all of this. When I think back on that now, I laugh because it was a little late to be thinking about being ready at that point. We talked about how we were going to tell our families the exciting news. Both our families knew we wanted children, but I think they figured it would take a while for me to actually get pregnant. So this news was going to be a bit of a shock.

Don asked me if everything was okay as far as me being pregnant. I told him that my doctor had referred me to a high-risk obstetrician at Akron General. I also told him that I had not called the doctor yet to set up the initial appointment. At first, he was concerned as to why my doctor had forwarded me to a high-risk doctor. He remembered me telling him that my doctor and I had discussed me getting pregnant in the past. Don remembered me saying that my doctor thought that I shouldn't have any problems but that he could not guarantee a successful pregnancy. I told him that my doctor referred me because a high-risk doctor would have more experience in dealing with complications that may occur in my pregnancy. Women with SCI (spinal cord injury) may be considered to have high risk pregnancies. However, I explained further that it does not mean that I would have complications. It simply meant that my doctor and I were taking precautions to prevent and treat complications if they did occur.

Additionally, the local hospital close to my home was not equipped to handle a high-risk pregnancy. Therefore, my doctor figured that it would be best if, from the early stages of the pregnancy, I be followed by the high-risk doctor. Also, this would ultimately be where I would deliver.

Why was I considered high-risk? There can be many complications that may result from a spinal cord injury. Inability to regulate blood pressure, low blood pressure, reduced control of body temperature, an inability to sweat that occurs below the level of injury, and chronic pain are only a few. Those issues, along with pregnancy, could place me and my baby at risk. After a long discussion about why my doctor wanted me to be seen by a high-risk doctor, Don and I were both very comfortable with his decision. Now we just needed to decide how we were going to tell our families.

I remember that we called Don's parents and told them our exciting news over the phone. Of course, they were very excited for us and could not wait to congratulate us in person. His parents were glad that I was feeling good and wanted to know when we had scheduled the first doctor's appointment. I had scheduled my appointment with my high-risk OB right after I had got off the phone with my doctor, so we were able to tell them when the appointment date was and that we would let them know how it all went.

Telling my mom was a different story. When it came to anything to do with me and any medical conditions that may have developed due to my injury, my mom was my lifeline. She was always there to listen to the doctors as they explained my symptoms and how they related to my spinal cord injury. She would then explain to me what the doctor meant, and she would make sure that everything the medical staff did was done right and that they understood my situation. She had been through so much with me, this injury, and overcoming this injury. I knew that telling her our news was going to be different. I knew she would be excited for Don and I, yet very nervous and fearful of what could happen to me throughout this pregnancy.

I had decided to tell her when she was at work. I figured that way she would be around medically knowledgeable individuals, so if she fainted, they could bring her to. Also, her co-workers at the hospital were, and still are, some of our close family friends, so I looked at telling her at work as two-fold—mom would know the news as well as a lot of other people that would need to be told. I wanted to tell her in a special and memorable way as well. So, instead of just showing up at her work and saying, *mom, guess what, you are going to be a grandma again,* I decided to send her flowers. Pink and blue carnations with a card that read, *"Dear Grandma, I cannot wait to meet you sometime in September, Love, Baby Frye."*

Well, when my mom got the flowers she was confused and puzzled at first as to why *she* would be receiving pink and blue flowers. It was necessary for her to read the card several times to understand what it said, and when she *did* get it, her colleagues told me she had to sit down and cry. She called me right after she got the flowers. She was very excited for Don and I, and in my mom's normal motherly fashion, she started firing off questions, asking what needed to be done next.

I explained to my mom that my regular OB had referred me to a high-risk OB specialist at Akron General Medical Center, and I asked if she would go with me to the first appointment. Don and I had already discussed that he really did not need to be there for the first appointment, but when we would find out the sex of the baby, he had to be there. Of course, my mom was all over coming with me.

Within a week of my OB doctor telling me that I was pregnant, I had an appointment with the high-risk doctor at Akron General. My appointment went well. I meet with the doctor in his office before he examined me. He explained to my mom and I that he had in fact delivered a baby to a paraplegic before, and that this woman had no problems. I remember assuming to myself that the woman, I was sure, had a cesarean birth. I was wrong. Again, what happens to the word "assume" when we break it down?

My doctor figured my due date would be around September 2nd. I thought that would be perfect. Let's go ahead and schedule the C-section for that day and move on to the examination. I remember saying to my doctor, "Do I schedule the C-section now or wait till the date gets closer?"

Looking at me oddly, he responded, "Why are you having a C-section?"

Now I started to question the title of high-risk doctor before this guy's name. I was asking myself, *exactly where did this guy go to medical school? Does he not see the wheelchair attached to my butt here? Did he misunderstand me saying that I am a quadriplegic, paralyzed? I mean, come on now, I need help going number two for gosh sake, and I am pretty sure that this child growing inside me was going to be bigger than my number two's!* (Again, I've given you too much information. But I knew you would want to know.)

My doctor went on, asking me a series of questions about my sensations in my abdomen. He asked if I could feel when I had menstrual cramps and if I could tell when I needed to go number two (I think that he may have used the medical term bowel movement, but I *so* think number two is cooler). My responses to his questions were yes, so he went on to explain that the female body is pretty amazing. And he also explained what it can do when getting a baby out. He would let me do all that my body would be able to do, and if I would need help, he would be there.

He went on to say he would possibly have to use forceps if I had trouble getting the baby's head out, or he would use a vacuum-type machine which more or less sucks onto the baby's head. I remember thinking at that point, *holy crap; I hope this guy is right,* because I was feeling very nervous. He had been talking about a whole lot of stuff and vacuuming, and I was thinking, *how am I going to get through this?* I had hundreds of questions racing through my head at this first doctor's appointment.

Before my doctor and I adjourned to the examination room, I was able to unleash several of the questions that were swirling around in my head: Can I drink Dr. Pepper? What about circulation in my legs as the baby grows? Will

I need to get off my butt more, meaning not sitting in my chair as much but lying down? He answered all my questions for the most part with yeses and nos and a lot of I-don't-know–we-will-take-it-a-day-at-a-times. He did say to me that I would need to be even more aware of my changing body, and that I would need to watch more diligently for any sores that would develop on my backside from the increased weight on my butt and legs while sitting.

Then we went to the examination room. My mom got me undressed and helped me transfer from my wheelchair to the examination table. I remember the nurse staying in the room in case my mom needed any help. Once on the table and situated, my doctor came back into the room and completed my exam. During my exam, my doctor asked my mom and I if twins ran in either side of the family. *Bullshit,* I remember thinking. I'm sorry for such language, and I know this is a family book, but *bullshit* on twins!

I remember my mom and I looking at each other, but, to be fair and honest here, I do not remember how my mom answered. My doctor went on to explain that my uterus felt bigger than seven weeks along, and he said than that he would like me to have an ultrasound done to make sure there was only one baby in there. I remember very little of my mom getting me redressed after the examination was done. I do remember the nurse stayed in the room again to assist my mom with getting me dressed and transferred off the table.

The whole time my mom and the nurse were getting me back into the chair, The nurse kept saying to not be alarmed by what the doctor said. She went on to say that he does this to a lot of the newly pregnant woman that he sees for the first time, saying that there may be more than one baby in there, and that most of the time he is wrong. Really?

I made the appointment for my ultrasound, and mom and I headed home that day. The whole way home I remember thinking, *twins? Seriously? How in the heck could I possibly be pregnant with two babies? If I thought before that taking care of one baby would be challenging and hard, now possibly two babies? And where were these children going to grow big in? Sure as H not my uterus!* I started to think than that I would probably have to be on bed rest pretty much my entire pregnancy!

I told Don the news when I got home, and at first, he did not believe me. Later that night, he started to talk about the what ifs. I remember him running through the list of pros and cons of having twins, with one pro being that I may only have to be pregnant once if it is a boy and a girl. Basically stating that I could get it all done at once. What's funny now, looking back on that whole pros and cons discussion, is that to this day I do not remember him stating one con. Luckily, after the ultrasound appointment and my doctor confirming that there was only one baby in there, the twin discussion dropped off. Except for Don's comments expressing how neat it may have been if we *did* have twins. (I would have figured a way for *him* to have carried them!)

Chapter Thirteen

I'm Pregnant!

My pregnancy went well. In the early stages, I remember coming home from work and wanting to go to bed. I remember feeling exhausted. My friend Barb would be at the house when I would come home from work to help me lay down. I would come home from work, she would be at my house waiting for me. I would come in, and she would help me use the restroom and then while she would be fixing dinner, I would usually lie in my bed on my left side and watch television. When Don would get home, Barb would transfer me back into my chair, and she would head home. Don and I would eat dinner, watch some TV, and then by eight to eight thirty, I was *out*. For the most part, my pregnancy was no different than an able-bodied pregnant woman's.

Then came the sickness. At about eight weeks into this pregnancy, like clockwork, from five until eight p.m., I was sick. I would eat, and within minutes after finishing, it would come back up. When Don and I would go out to dinner, we would take a bucket and a roll of paper towels.

When I got back into my van to leave, I would throw-up, wipe my mouth, and we would head home. Talk about wasting money on a dinner date!

Luckily, the sick, throwing-up feeling only lasted maybe four weeks, but that was plenty for me to have the experience of pregnancy sickness. One of my very dear, *tall* friends was sick her entire pregnancy, and I cannot even imagine going through that. (Her height had nothing to do with her being sick, either; it's just a way to identify her without saying her name.)

After the sickness subsided, my pregnancy was smooth sailing. I did experience dizziness and lightheadedness as the baby grew, and I had to be very aware of this, especially when I was driving. There was one time when I was driving over to my mom's house, by myself, and I remember that when I got there I told my mom that I felt dizzy. She took my blood pressure (what good nurse doesn't have a blood pressure cuff laying around?), and it was something like seventy over forty.

Of course, I do not need to say that this blood pressure reading caused a bit of alarm in my mom. She had me call the doctor's office, and they told me to lie down, preferably on my left side, and retake it. I lay down on my left side, and mom did just that. It had improved a little but was still low.

At my next appointment, I talked with my doctor about this issue. He did not appear alarmed about it happening, but he told me to be careful driving and that if it got worse, it may come down to me not being able to drive further along in my pregnancy. Luckily, I did not lose my driving privileges during the pregnancy, but what I did end up losing was the luxury of being at home the last five or so weeks of it.

At about twenty-seven weeks, I experienced Braxton Hicks, aka, false labor. I had been at my job that morning and felt something different in my stomach. I remember leaning over a bit when I first felt it, but when I would try to sit up straight, I felt this sort of grabbing sensation in my stomach. I also felt immediate panic. There was no way that this baby was ready to be born.

An ambulance came to my work and took me to the local hospital, where I was checked-out in the emergency room to determine if I was in labor. The ER doctor thought it was just false labor or ligaments stretching in my belly, but my doctor sent me up to labor and delivery to put me on monitors for a couple hours just to make sure nothing was brewing down there.

After about three hours of lying there, it was determined that I was not contracting and it would be safe for me to go home. My doctor told me to lie down, again on my left side, and take it easy. Once we got home, I asked Don to get me Taco Bell (I had been craving tacos and watermelon my entire pregnancy), and we spent a quiet evening at home taking it easy.

For the next several weeks, my pregnancy went smoothly. My stomach was growing, my boobs were getting huge, and Don was really starting to like my new changing body. (I will let you all figure out for yourselves his favorite changing part.) I still had to spend time lying down, though.

My legs would swell from the weight of the baby pressing down on my leg veins. Since my circulation was already affected by the spinal injury, the weight of the baby on my leg veins impaired my circulation even more. A danger that I had to be more aware of while I was pregnant was blood clots. With the weight of the baby resting on my legs, the circulation of the blood in my legs was more constricted, increasing the danger of me developing blood clots.

On top of the circulation and possible blood clot danger, sitting was starting to get increasingly uncomfortable. With sitting all the time, the baby really had nowhere to grow but up, which meant encroaching on my stomach and lungs. When I would stretch out and lay on my side in bed, it was more comfortable to breathe and eat.

I never felt inconvenienced by the obstacles of my pregnancy because to me, just being pregnant was a blessing, and knowing that the end result would be me having my baby got me through it. I will say one thing: having a spinal injury and going through the recovery process of this injury teaches a person a huge lesson in patience. I think a person with a spinal injury learns the true definition of what it means to wait for things. Whether that means waiting for food, drink, or even getting dressed. They learn, by no choice of their own, to survive with this new lifestyle. Some days it is easier than others to be patient. I will say that over time, it became easier. The patience I used during my pregnancy was well worth it. I knew I was not going to be pregnant forever, and in the end, I would give birth to my child. Plus, for me, lying in bed a couple hours a day was a piece of cake compared to lying in bed for two months in traction.

My doctor had scheduled me for an ultrasound at the twenty-week mark because both Don and I wanted to know the sex of the baby. It did not matter to us what we were having, but we both wanted to know if it was a boy or girl. Don and I had found out that this little bundle that was growing and flipping around inside of me was a Maxwell Hamilton.

Early in the pregnancy, I would have sworn on everything that I believed in that was holy that I was carrying a girl. I don't know why I thought this, but for some reason, I just kept feeling it was a girl. Thank God it was a boy! Again, not because we wouldn't be excited for a girl or that I felt some obligation to give Don a boy, but more so because we couldn't agree on a girl's name! We kicked around Emma Jane, Jane after my mom's middle name, but Don was not real keen on that. We talked about Adeline, after Don's grandmother, and that one was holding strong between the two of us.

When I had the ultrasound done, I will never forget when the technician scanned that wand over my belly, and sure enough, Adeline was out. It was a Maxwell Hamilton. Don and I had both picked this name even *before* we had got pregnant. The name Hamilton is Don's and his dad's middle name. And Don and I both just loved the name Max.

So, from that ultrasound appointment on, Don and I would always refer to the baby as Max. And let me just say, Max was an active little one. I remember the first time I felt him move, well I should say, *really* felt it. Early in the pregnancy, around the tenth through the twentieth week, I remember feeling little flutters and twinges, but it was at about twenty-seven weeks that I could really feel him moving around.

For some reason, Max would curl up in a ball and move far to the left side of my belly (probably because I spent so much time lying *on* my left side). He would do this mainly in the evening, and Don would have to push on my belly to get him to move back to the center. It was the freakiest looking thing, too. I could be lying in bed on my back, and all of a sudden, my stomach would start to move, and off to the left side he would go. It was almost alien-like! I was so thankful, though, to be able to *feel* him moving that I did not care if it *did* look alien-like. I could *feel* my little alien moving inside me!

Don and I begun prepping the nursery. I was thirty weeks along and had had two baby showers already. I was so excited to get everything washed and in its place so we could just relax for the last several weeks and get ready for boy-wonder to come into the world.

My mom and Barb were a huge help in getting everything washed and ready to be put away. Don had painted the room a Nantucket Blue color and a good friend of mine was going to come paint some animals on the nursery walls. Since we did not have a theme for the nursery, Don and I thought a giraffe painted on one wall with his long neck extending over to the next wall would be cute. My friend painted the giraffe in a whimsical way, and it looked like it was looking down into Max's crib. On the other wall, she painted a big tree that went up onto the ceiling. In the tree were two whimsical monkeys in colorful striped shirts. The coolest thing, though, was how she made the tree trunk look like it had "Max" carved into it with his date of birth.

I loved his nursery! It was emotionally hard let go of that room when we ended up selling our house. I am not sure if I was in denial that Max would ever think about changing his room someday, as he grew older. What I did know and was holding onto then was that Max would be the first college freshman with a giraffe looking into his bed when he'd come home on his breaks.

It was during this time that I also decided that all the carpet needed to come out of our house and new, clean, fresh carpet put down. Why? If you remember, Don put a tremendous amount of work into our home by renovating the bathrooms, painting, and putting up bead board in our kitchen and dining room area. The one thing we did not do, though, was replace any of the flooring. Yes, we did put new flooring in the two baths, but the rest was what was in when we bought the house. Now, since my first child was going to come home to this house, everything had to be clean and new. Talk about nesting when you are pregnant!

So, since we were painting and turning the spare room into the nursery, we decided to replace all the carpeting in the house. My thought was also that eventually, this child of ours would be crawling on the floor. There was no way *my* child, my alien-like baby, was going to crawl on this *filthy* disgusting carpeting! So Don tore out all the carpeting over the weekend, and the carpet installers were scheduled to come the following week to install our new clean carpet. I was starting my thirty-second week of being pregnant.

Chapter Fourteen

Preterm Labor

I had been at work all day the day I went into premature labor. Throughout the day, my stomach had been bothering me, but I thought nothing of it and figured that when I got home, I would lay down for a while. I certainly did not think that I was in labor!

When I got home, my friend Barb was there to help me go to the bathroom and change out of my work clothes. It was almost mid-July, and the weather was beautiful. My mom was coming over for the evening to stay with me because Don had set up to go night fishing with a good buddy of his. My mom had planned to mow our grass while she was over because my mother loves to mow.

I had told my husband, as he was getting all his fishing gear together, to make sure he took his cell phone and to make sure to keep it on. See, my husband has a tendency to not really worry about whether you can get a hold of him or not. He will often say, "I do not live my life by my phone." Which I agree with–to a point. The point being, if your quadriplegic wife is home and thirty-two weeks pregnant, I would have to say this would be a time to live by your phone!

Don said to me as he was leaving our home that early July evening, "Barb, nothing is going to happen, you will be fine. Besides, you're not due for eight more weeks." And off he went. The only thing I knew was that he was going to Mogadore Lake in Portage County.

My mom had started mowing, and Barb and I were starting the process of helping me go to the bathroom. As we were doing this, my friend noticed that there was blood after I had peed. Needless to say, my friend freaked out! She ran outside to get my mom off the mower, and when my mom saw the blood, she told me to call my doctor. I called Dr. Stewart's office, and since it was after business hours, I was sent to his pager phone. Within minutes after leaving him a message, he called me back and told me to go to Akron General Hospital's Labor and Delivery Department and get checked out. My mom and I loaded up in the van, and off we went to Akron General. On the way, I tried calling Don to let him know what was going on, but of course, his phone was turned off. At that point, I was not too concerned because I was thinking that this trip to Akron General was no big deal, and I was sure that Labor and Delivery would just tell me everything was okay and send me home.

My mom and I arrived at the hospital and went straight to Labor and Delivery. Dr. Stewart had called the department ahead of time, so they knew I was coming in and what symptoms I was experiencing. They took me to an examination room, and my mom and another nurse got me on the table. They undressed me from the waist down, and I waited for the doctor to come in. Within minutes, one of the resident doctors came in and introduced himself and said that he had spoken with Dr. Stewart and that he was going to do an internal on me to make sure everything was okay. I will say, at this point I was not scared or alarmed at anything going on because I had internals before during this pregnancy, and everything turned out fine. So to me, an internal exam was just going to assure Dr. Stewart that everything was still okay.

Well, everything was not okay. The resident doctor determined from the exam that I was two centimeters dilated and fifty percent effaced. In other words, I was in premature labor. I was panicked! My mind was racing. I remember thinking, *it is too early for me to be in labor. My baby is not ready to come out!*

I started to cry when I heard the doctor say I was in labor. *Oh my gosh, my baby! My Max. He is going to be too little to survive.* My mom was right there, and she assured me that everything would be okay, and she said it was good that we had come to the hospital because the doctors and nurses knew what to do. It was decided that I would be admitted to the hospital that night, because either of two things were going to happen. One, my son was going to be born eight weeks early and weighing in at just two pounds. Two, my doctor was going to try to stop my labor. The goal was obviously the second option, but they did prepare me for the first.

While the resident and nurses were attending to my needs, my mom was frantically try to get a hold of Don, whose phone was still off. My mom called my sister and brother-in-law and told them what was happening. My sister and brother-in-law immediately came up to the hospital to be with me and my mom and to help in the pursuit of locating my loving husband. (Do you sense my sarcastic tone here?) My brother-in-law asked me what lake Don was fishing on, and he said that he would try to contact a ranger in that particular park.

In the meantime, I was moved over to a more private room on the Labor and Delivery floor, and an IV was started with a drug that would hopefully stop, or at least lessen, my contractions. I could not feel my contractions very much due to the paralysis. What I could feel was my stomach tightening and then releasing, so I knew when I was having a contraction. Also, the nurses had put monitors on my stomach. One monitor detected when a contraction was happening, and another monitored Max's heart beat. I was able to hear Max's little heart rate, which sounded like water swishing to a beat. It was somewhat reassuring to hear his heart swishing away, but also scary, because I feared that he would be born too early. I was told that night that he had a fifty percent chance of survival. I started to pray over and over in my head, *please Lord, keep my baby inside me as long as possible!*

Besides the IV drugs they were giving me to slow down my contractions, I also received steroid shots in my thigh to push along Max's lung development. My mom had called Don's parents to alert them to what was going on, and they came to the hospital that night as well.

They first started me on Terbutaline, a medication used to stop premature labor. This medication made my heart race and made me physically sick. My mom had advised them not to use any type of drug that had a bronchodilator in it because I had had adverse reactions to similar medications in the past. Well, apparently the medical staff thought my mom did not know what she was talking about and administered Terbutaline anyway.

I did become violently sick, and I thought my heart was going to beat out of my chest. The medical staff now saw that my mom was not overreacting about not giving me Terbutaline. They consulted with my doctor, and it was decided that they try a different medication. I was then put on Magnesium Sulfate, another labor-stopping drug.

As this was all going on, my brother-in-law was trying to locate Don. Now I was starting to panic. A nurse had come into my room to go over paperwork to cover what could happen. She discussed with me that if my labor were to continue, I would deliver in the operating room. Max would most likely be taken immediately over to Akron Children's Neonatal Unit because of his size and underdeveloped lungs. Akron Children Hospital is located just a block or two from Akron General and has one of the best NICU's around. As the nurse was giving me all of this information, I couldn't stop thinking about Don. I needed my husband there with me, and I was praying, *Dear Lord, please let my baby survive.*

The nurse also had to cover the really bad and scary stuff. If my baby were not to survive, did we want our own clergy present to baptize the baby or the hospital's clergyman that was on staff? I saw the nurse's mouth move as she was explaining these thing, but all I could think about was, *Dear God, please do not take my baby.* I signed papers saying that I understood what the nurse had just gone over with me. These papers stated that if the baby, Max, as he was to me already, did not survive, then we would have him baptized. I mindlessly signed them, but nothing was really registering in my head. *He had to be okay*, I kept telling myself. *My baby had to be okay.*

In the meantime, Scott, my brother-in-law, was able to get a hold of a ranger that was on duty at the lake. Scott told him the situation– this guy's wife was in pre-mature labor, and he needed to get to the hospital. He explained that it was a medical emergency and how obviously important it was to find him.

Because the lake that Don was fishing on was huge, with several boat docks, it was by pure luck that the ranger was able to locate him. It would almost be like finding a teenager in a mall without a cell phone—in other words, impossible. Scott gave the ranger a description of Don's truck and said that Don and his buddy would most likely be out on the lake in Don's boat rather than fishing from shore.

Don ended up getting to the hospital around one a.m. I updated him on what all had been done, and I explained to him that I was on an IV medication which would hopefully stop my contractions. I told him that Max had a fifty percent chance of survival if he was born that night, and I remember the look on his face as I said those words. He looked terrified.

Don stayed the night with me, and in the morning, Dr. Stewart came in to check on me. The IV medication had slowed my contractions down, which was a good sign. The bad thing, though, was that one of the side effects of this drug was paralysis. Seriously, *paralysis*. This drug they had me on virtually paralyzed me from about the face down. Okay, maybe not the face, but I will say, while on this drug, I could only see someone if they were directly in front of my hospital bed. If they moved to either side, I could not get my eyes to follow their movement. As that was happing, Dr. Stewart became aware of the fact that they may need to drop my dose down a bit. Dr. Stewart explained that this drug somewhat paralyzes the uterus, which in theory stops it from contracting. Well, along with the uterus, it can affect the ability to raise one's arms, as well as one's breathing. And for me, it even affected the peripheral muscle in my eyes, which is why I could not move my eyes from side to side.

Dr. Stewart cut back on the amount of Magnesium Sulfate I was receiving, and everything seemed to calm down for that moment. I was kept on the Labor and Delivery floor for several days until a room opened up on their peri-natal wing. If the medication could stop my contractions until I reached my 36th week of pregnancy, Dr. Stewart felt that Max's lungs would be more developed.

I understood that it was the most desirable scenario for him to stay inside of me as long as possible, but I was only thinking, *oh my gosh, I have to be in the hospital till I am thirty-six weeks along? That is a month! I have spent thirteen months in a hospital and now you want me to do a month... Again? Why can't I go home and lay in my own bed for a month? My mom's a nurse, she will take care of me.*

As long as I was having contractions, Dr. Stewart said it would be too risky to have me home on bed rest. If I were to actually go into full labor, he did not want to risk anything happening to me or Max. I understood what he was saying, but I was still not happy about having to be in the hospital on bed rest for a month. Dr. Stewart topped the conversation off with, "Let's hope you go to thirty-seven or thirty-eight weeks. Or even forty weeks, because that would assure that Max had plenty of cooking time." *Really? Are you serious?* I was absolutely not in the mood to hear that news. Don kept reassuring me that I would want what is best for Max. The longer I could keep him inside me, the better it would be for him. Yes, I understood all this, but I was still hypersensitive to long hospital stays!

About a week into my stay, I developed a fever. I was taken for an ultrasound to determine if I had developed a clot somewhere. They scanned my legs first. Because I had only been lying in bed and because of my spinal cord injury, my chances for developing a blood clot were high. Also, with the weight of the baby pressing down on my legs and groin veins, my circulation was compromised even more.

Luckily, there were no clots found in my legs. Now they needed to see what else could be the cause for my fever. They scheduled a chest X-ray to look at my lungs. There was the answer: the lower part of one of my lungs was collapsed. It was determined that I had developed pneumonia.

It was a relief that I did not have a blood clot. Dr. Stewart put me on Heparin shots to help reduce my chances of developing a clot as well as antibiotics for the pneumonia. Also, he decided to take me off the Magnesium Sulfate. In my opinion, he realized that the Mag, as it is referred to in medical terminology, may have played a part in the development of pneumonia. The Mag seemed to paralyze my insides; therefore, my breathing was affected by the drug.

Even though hospitals are supposed to be the best place to be when a person is sick or hurt, they can also be the most germ-infested place a person can be. It was determined that I probably caught an airborne pneumonia germ, and we were hopeful that the IV antibiotics would wipe it out. Since Dr. Stewart took me off the Mag, keeping my contractions under control was still a priority, so he put me on Procardia, a cardiac drug, and it seemed to work. I still contracted about every seven to ten minutes, but the Procardia seemed to prevent me from dilating past the two centimeters that I was at when I was first admitted.

I was still on the monitors, one for my contractions and one for Max's heart rate. I was moved over to the perinatal unit at Akron General and given my own room. The room was meant for two patients, but the nursing staff was very considerate and gave me a private room because of all the space I took up. I had my power wheelchair there, and Don was able to spend the night in the extra bed.

My room was at the end of the hall with two big corner windows. There were pros and cons to being near these windows. The life-flight helicopter pad was outside my window, and it was exciting to watch it come and go. It helped pass the time a little better. On the other hand, it was sad, because life-flight meant trauma or a critical patient. Yes, watching life-flight come and go was a change from staring at day-time television, but I would always say a silent prayer for the injured or sick person on the flight as well as their family.

It was mid July when I was admitted to the hospital. In fact, it was July 10th, to be exact. So having the two big windows to look outside was also a perk because, as every Northern Ohioan knows, July is one of the sunniest and warmest months we get. After my second week or so in the hospital, Dr. Stewart felt it would be okay for me to get up in my wheelchair and go outside in the evening when Don was there.

Don would transfer me into my chair and we would first head to the cafeteria so he could get some dinner. From the cafeteria, we would either go outside and sit in the courtyard or (this is what I liked to do) go down to the nursery and see the newborn babies. I secretly hoped that if Max heard the sounds of the babies crying, he would want to venture on out of that uterus of mine and join the crowd. Yes, I know that was not the best thing to wish, but I was still in the poor-me-for-having-to-be-in-the-hospital pity party. In time, that would be changing. I just didn't know it.

As I have explained before, the longer a person's stay is in a hospital, the closer they become to the medical staff. Additionally, one gets to hear the stories from the rooms beyond his or her little hospital room walls. On the perinatal unit, most patients are there because they are pregnant, obviously, and it is either a high-risk pregnancy, as mine was, or they have developed complications during their pregnancy. Come to find out, there were other pregnant woman way worse off in their pregnancy than I was. Therefore, I started to stop feeling sorry for myself and started to realize that things could be worse.

After hearing the stories of the other women who were on bed rest and about how long they had already been on bed rest, I started to reevaluate my this-is-not-fair attitude. I quickly realized that I was on bed rest so my son would have a better chance of survival. It was then that I actually realized that I was going to be a mom. Did my mom think it was not fair that her daughter suffered a broken neck and was now a quadriplegic? My mom never felt it was unfair. She unselfishly gave up *years* of her life to help me recover from my injury. She felt grateful that I was still alive, and whatever she had to give up or do, she did with a joyful and grateful spirit. She's a mom, and that's what moms do.

I did have a lot of thinking time while I waited for Max to grow inside me. At night, I would think about all the care that this baby would need. Feeding, bathing, changing. *How am I going to handle watching someone bath my son? Is my son going to recognize me as his mom? What if he does not bond with me?* I remember literally lying there at night, freaking myself out by just *thinking* about all this stuff. When my mom would come in during the day, I would be a basket case. My mom would of course reassure me that babies know their moms regardless of whether they are the ones changing them, feeding them, or doing whatever else. She also reminded me that, for the past eight and a half months, it has been my voice which Max has been hearing. I would always feel reassured after mom and I had our talks.

After begging Dr. Stewart for three weeks, he finally agreed to letting me *try* to go home and continue on bed rest. We were still looking at possibly four more weeks until my due date, and I was starting to lose my newly found positive attitude about being on bed rest. I think I wore him down so much by repeatedly asking him if I could try to go home that he just finally gave in and said yes. I later found out that he knew it would not work out, and sure enough, he was right.

I got to go home for four hours. Dr. Stewart referred to it as my "little field trip." I arrived home and immediately got into my bed, and wow, did that feel so good. My own bed. It's amazing how we take for granted such little things. I was given a list of medications that needed to be filled, so Don was off to fill the scripts. My good friend Barb stayed with me, and if I were to describe her as being a nervous wreck, I would be downplaying how she really felt about being left alone with me. She stood at the edge of my bed, staring at me and threatening that if I went into labor, she was going to quit working for me. Her words didn't come as a shock to me because her threat to quit had been an ongoing joke. When things got crazy, she'd say she was quitting. At last count, she had quit working for me thirty eight times.

One requirement of my trip home was that I had to hook up to a monitor pack and keep an eye on my contractions for a half hour or so. Once done, I would then have to call a number, press in a code, and the monitor device that I had hooked up could be read by a medical office somewhere. By the time Don got back from getting some groceries, filling my prescriptions, and stopping to get a movie we could watch, the medical office had called me to see how I was feeling. My monitor apparently showed that in forty-five minutes, I had had eleven contractions. I told her that I felt fine, but she said that considering the high-risk situation, she felt it would be best that I return to the hospital. I was a little bummed, I will admit, but I thought being home for four hours was better than nothing.

It was not to long after my field trip, maybe a week or so, that I had reached the thirty-six week mark of my pregnancy. Dr. Stewart decided that he was going to take me off of the medication which had been keeping me from going into full labor and send me home until that happened. He explained that according to ultrasound pictures, Max was at a good, viable size to survive just fine outside of the womb. He also went on to say that I could continue to labor like I had been for the last five weeks, but when I start to feel things really change and feel different, I better high tail it into Labor & Delivery.

I listened to everything he said and promised him that I would follow his instructions. I was going home. I remember thinking, *the next time I come back to this hospital it would be for the real thing, and I will be leaving with my son in my arms*. That was one thing I found amazing. A woman and man can be admitted to the hospital as a couple and leave as a family. That never gets old, does it? It's a miracle.

Chapter Fifteen

Max

I spent five whole days at home this time before my contractions started to feel different and more uncomfortable. Until this point, I knew I was having contractions, and I could feel my stomach harden and relax, but I never really had pain or discomfort. This time I felt discomfort and most definitely some pain.

The date was August 12th, and it was a beautiful, sunny day. Don had gone to work that day because there was no sense in him staying home and staring at me. We wanted to save all of his time for when I had Max. There had been several different false alarm trips throughout my five-week stay in the hospital. I would call him at work and say it's time, the contractions are quite strong. He would drive from his office in Cleveland down to Akron just for me to say, "Nope, not today." So my mom again had come to stay wit me while Don went off to work. I also had my good friends Nancy and Barb coming over to help me, so I was covered as far as my care.

My mom had started to mow the grass again that day (I am starting to see the pattern of my mom mowing and me going to the hospital), and I remember flagging her down in the front yard and telling her that I felt strange. Of course, she immediately got off the tractor and started asking me questions. She asked me when my last contraction was and instructed me to tell her when the next one was starting so she could time it. After thirty minutes, she and I decided to call Dr. Stewart, and sure enough, we were headed back to Akron General.

My mom gathered my bag and everything else we had laid out to take–video cam and baby book (so I could get his footprints stamped in it). I called Don and told him that we were heading back to the hospital because my contractions seemed to be intensifying, and I did not want to risk anything. Can I tell you too what my wonderful, supportive, selfish, inconsiderate husband said to me when I told him this? *Was I sure?* Was I sure this time, because the past several times were false alarms, and he reminded me that I was still not quiet thirty-seven weeks along. Here's the selfish, inconsiderate part: He had told me that he was planning on coming home from work that day to take a nap because I had got him up several times throughout the night to help me reposition. Poor guy was really tired. *Really?*

My response to him was that I was so sorry the pending birth of our child was going to interrupt his napping! (By the way, my tone while saying this was sarcastic–but I really did mean it.) I told him that I would call him when I got to the hospital and let him know what was going on. Looking back, I think I seriously thought about not calling him and letting him *nap* through the birth of his son. (Kidding! Pregnant women get very sarcastic and irritable the last several weeks!)

My mom and I arrived at the hospital, and I was admitted onto the Labor and Delivery floor. It was about two to two thirty in the afternoon, and I was immediately hooked up to the monitors. Sure enough, I was contracting, but within forty-five minutes of getting hooked up, the contractions stopped. Bull crap, I remember thinking. Okay, maybe not crap; I'm sure I used much more forceful language.

One of the resident doctors that I had really enjoyed talking with during my five-week bed rest stint was on that day in Labor and Delivery. I remember saying to him that I was not leaving this hospital again until I had my son in my arms. He assured me that we would wait a little bit to see what happened, and sure enough, the contractions started back up. Don was hoping that he was going to be able to sneak home and get a nap in before heading up to the hospital, but no such luck. I told him this was the real deal and to get to the hospital.

My mom called everyone she knew, and Don called his mom and dad. My IV was started, and now we just needed to wait for Max to make his appearance. I was hoping to be able to hold off birth until morning because Dr. Stewart was not on duty that night. I really, really wanted Dr. Stewart to deliver my baby. Don't get me wrong. The other doctors in practice with Dr. Stewart where just as good. I had just seen Dr. Stewart the most throughout my pregnancy, and he and I had really bonded. So, when I heard Dr. Stewart was due back on duty at 8 a.m. Wednesday morning, I knew I had to hold out.

It was about three in the morning when they started me on Pitocin, an IV drug commonly used to progress labor. I had made it to seven centimeters but had stalled out there for several hours. I was consistently contracting, but nothing was happening. I asked the nurse how long it would be before I would feel the effects of the Pitocin, and she said within a couple hours.

In the meantime, a fold out bed had been brought into my room, and Don was fast asleep on that throughout the night. My mom and Mrs. Frye had stayed up with me to keep me company and help make the time go by faster. I believe Mr. Frye had excused himself to the L & D waiting room and had fallen asleep.

I was never so glad to see Dr. Stewart's face poke around that door first thing Wednesday morning, and the only thing he said was, "Barb, you are lucky." What he meant was that he wanted to be as much of a part of this birth as all of us. He and I had many talks throughout my pregnancy about the birth, and I made him promise me that he had to be on call when I went into full labor. Of course, he would say, "Don't have this baby until I am on call." I remember we would laugh about it, but deep down we both knew it meant a lot to the both of us that he deliver my baby.

It was now Wednesday, August 13th, and I had been in good labor for about six or so hours. Dr. Stewart checked me to see how far along I had progressed on the Pitocin, and I had only moved to eight centimeters. He felt, at that point, that my bowels were full, preventing Max from moving down into the birth canal. Getting my bowels cleaned out would hopefully cause me to dilate more. (Yes, pregnancy and labor and delivery talk is sometimes gross and weird, but it's a fact of life.) I was rolled over to be placed on the bed pan to see if I could go. Just as they rolled me over, my water broke, and it was go time! Immediately after that, I dilated to ten centimeters, and it was time to deliver.

I was in labor! Within minutes my bed, like a transformer, turned into a labor chair, and Dr. Stewart was telling me to push. My mom was still in the room on one side of me, and Don was on the other side of the bed, rubbing my head. A big table, where Max would be put once he arrived, was wheeled into the room. There, they would weigh him and clean him all up before we would get to hold him.

Dr. Stewart was in place along with a resident doctor who had been following my pregnancy. Her name totally escapes me, but I remember she was super sweet. I really enjoyed the times she spent with me when she would do her rounds. Oh yeah, back to my delivery. There were several nurses now coming in and out of the room getting everything ready.

I remember asking the nurse for my epidural. I *needed* my epidural. I had studied this magic shot during Lamaze, and dog gone it, I was gonna get it. It would take the pain away. I remember repeatedly asking for my epidural. The nurses were telling me that the entire staff of doctors that administer epidurals were busy. *Are you flipping kidding me?* I remember thinking. *Busy? This is Akron General Medical Center. There has to be a bajillion doctors that give epidurals in this hospital, and you are telling me that they are all busy?*

What I later found out was that the nurses *and* my mom knew it was too late for an epidural, so they basically lied to me to calm me down. That, or to shut me up. Dr. Stewart stepped in and said that it was too late to get the epidural; I needed to try to push the best I could.

Before I go on, let me describe my labor pains once fully dilated. My contractions were really kicked in, and every contraction made me feel like my head was going to explode. It was like the worst ever migraine headache times infinity, plus one. When the contraction would subside, the pain in my head would ease up. Of course, once one contraction was ending another was starting up. I felt like I was dying. I felt like I was having a stroke and was never going to see the birth of my son. I was even screaming out, "I am having a stroke!" Dr. Stewart reassured me that I was not having a stroke, but it was indeed time to push this baby out.

Don wanted just me and him to be present at the birth of Max. I will be honest here; with no disrespect to my husband *at all*, a part of me wanted my mom there with me. My mom had been through *so* much with me but knew it meant a lot to Don. Therefore, when it came time to push, my mom stepped out in the hall and joined Mr. and Mrs. Frye.

A nurse was on one side of me, and Don was on the other. They both locked arms with me to help me sit up and push. As I was sitting up pushing, Dr. Stewart reached up with his forearm and kind of swept down on my belly. We did this again, but before the second push, Dr. Stewart used forceps to pop Max's head out. On the second push, out he came. At 10:44 a.m., August 13th, 1998, Maxwell Hamilton Frye made his way into this world, and even more than I ever could have imagined–into my heart!

It was the most incredible feeling in the world. I had never felt a love like this before. I could not believe how much I could love something. My son was perfect. I just kept looking over at him as they were cleaning him up, and I was so happy to see his arms and legs moving. I knew there was no chance that my paralysis could be passed on to him, but I was still so relieved so see all his limbs moving.

Max weighed seven pounds eleven ounces and was twenty-one inches long. Not a bad sized baby for being three weeks early. After Dr. Stewart and the resident doctor got Max and I cleaned up, everyone came back into the room. I started to have some issues with my blood pressure elevating and dropping, so Dr. Stewart gave me some oxygen while having me lay flat for a while.

We stayed in the L & D room for a while, waiting for a bed to be ready on the maternity floor. It was mid-afternoon before we got moved to our room, and Don and I decided we would rest for an hour or two and send Max to the nursery. Don and I were both exhausted from being up most the night. Well, I should say *I* was up all night; Don got several little naps in.

We lasted about fifteen or twenty minutes into our nap before we both could not take it anymore–we had to go get our son. Having waited long enough to see him and hold him, Don ended up going to get him from the nursery and bring him back to the room.

Max was such a little peanut when he was born. I remember that I would just sit there and stare at him for hours. I couldn't believe that he was mine. I had a child–a perfect baby boy. If someone would have said to me while

I was laying with screws in my skull to stabilize my broken neck that fourteen years from then, I would be at the most incredible time of my life birthing my child, I would have said no way. And there I was, holding this incredible gift from God. I was so thankful for my life.

With the birth of my son, it also made me realize how much a parent loves their child and worries about them. One day as I was watching Max sleep in his bassinet, I remember thinking that I would absolutely die if anything happened to this child. I would sit there and look at him and think that he was my whole world. That love I felt for Max, and still do, made me aware of what my parents must have felt the night they got that horrible call from the hospital. My mom shared with me later that she felt so helpless that night because there was nothing she could do to make me better. I still carry guilt from the choice I made that night.

After a three day stay in the hospital, Dr. Stewart discharged me. Don and I could not wait to get our little guy home to his new house. With both of our families waiting for our arrival home, everyone ended up over at our house to welcome the newest member.

Don had a week off to be home with me and Max. He wanted it to be just us three that week, so we could bond and be a family. Well, he made it about three days until he was asking if my mom could come over and stay. He had been getting up throughout the night when Max would cry and bring Max to me because I was breast-feeding. But it was not like he could just hand Max off to me and go back and lay down. Don had to fully help me feed Max.

It was easiest for me to feed him lying on my side. Don would help me roll on my side, and then he would have to position Max in front of me. Don would then lay behind me until I had to switch sides. One time Don had got me situated and got Max latched on, eating. He lay down behind me and fell asleep. Well, I had fallen asleep as well. All of a sudden, I woke up, looked down, and could not find Max! I quickly nudged Don and moved the blanket away. Max had wiggled down in bed and was sucking on my stomach! Poor kid!

After three days of getting up during the night and helping with feeding, Don decided that we had all the rest of this kid's life to bond. He needed to sleep. So my mom and Mrs. Frye stayed with us for a while. All in all, the transition of getting Max home and settled went very smoothly.

I spent six months at home with Max before I returned to work at my job with the county. I loved every minute of being home with him. Max spent very little time in his crib for naps because I just wanted to constantly keep him near me. I was forever kissing him. Of course, I was kissing him because he was the cutest baby in the world. But I was also kissing him because I could feel him the best with my lips. My lips were not paralyzed, so I could feel his skin and how soft it was. I could feel how warm he was—or wasn't. I constantly had my lips on him or his little fingers or toes on my face.

Let me explain this further. I could feel Max with my hands, but as far as the real fine feelings—softness, warmth, smoothness—I could not feel that. I could not feel the softness of my son nor the warmth of his little body. One time, I remember Don was changing him, and I told Don to put Max's bum by my face. Of course, I asked this after he wiped him really well, but I wanted to feel his bum and his little back against my skin, the skin where I could feel the most. Oh, how we take so much for granted. I am sure most parents don't put their faces up against their baby's bottoms.

I do have to say, I still today feel his skin with my face. No I do not put his cute, little toes on my face anymore simply because those cute toes have turned into stinky, sweaty fourteen-year-old feet! (I will say though, they are still cute!) And Lord only knows what his bum has sat in now! But as Max grew, I constantly would be kissing on him—just to feel the chubby, softness of his skin.

As far as Max's care, I had my good friends Nancy and Barb who worked for me. I had hired additional girls that would help as well, but mainly Nancy, Barb, Don, and both families helped me with his care. I went back to work when Max was six months old. Nancy would come to my house in the morning to help me get up and dressed for work. When I was ready, Max would start stirring in his crib, so Nancy and I would go in together and get my little guy up. It meant a lot to me that when he saw my face, he would identify me as his mom. All the girls that worked for me knew how much that meant to me, so they always made sure to place Max where he could see me when they were changing him or dressing him. I would talk to him during that time and tell him how much mommy loves him. There was no doubt that he knew who his mommy was.

After Nancy and I got Max changed and dressed and his bag packed, I would give him a big kiss good-bye and I would head to work. Nancy would then load Max up in her car and take him to her house to watch him during the day. This continued until Max was almost three years old. When Max turned three, we started him in a two day a week preschool. Don would drop him off in the morning and I would pick him up after work. The ladies at his preschool would help me get Max to the car and buckle him into his car seat. When I would get home, my friend Barb would already be at my house, so she would help get Max out. We had an awesome system going.

Max, for the most part, was an awesome baby and toddler. One of the many fears that I had about being a mom was the thought of having a child who was a runner. We all know the ones. I remember seeing moms in stores, and they would be trying everything possible to control their children. Then all of a sudden, the kid would just dart right out of mom's reach. I remember thinking, *good Lord, what would I do if my child ran from me? I guess I could chase him down in my wheelchair and try to cut him off.* Kind of sounds like cattle herding, doesn't it? Luckily, Max was not a runner.

As Max got older and I could take him more places by myself, he got to the point where he could undo his car seat and get out of it on his own. I would then have him either climb up onto my lap, or I would have a place on the back of my wheelchair where he would climb up and hold on. It was the cutest thing ever. People would constantly stop me and say what a good boy he was.

One time when Max was older, maybe four or five, he and I were grocery shopping. I had to pick up a few things, and Max loved to be mommy's helper. Throughout our shopping adventure, Max had been talking to me, pointing to things and asking me questions. He was saying, "Mom, what's that? Mom, what's this?" I noticed a woman standing not too far away from us, and I could tell she was taking in our whole conversation. Within a few minutes, the woman came up to me and commented that he was such a good boy. She also commented on the uncanniness of how much he looked like me for an adopted child! Had I not had my seat belt on, I would have fallen out of my chair. Wow! I looked at the lady with total shock on my face, and I simply responded with, "Oh no, he's from me."

The look on the woman's face was of complete embarrassment, and she tried to backpedal her way out by saying more idiotic statements. I just smiled and called for Max, my biological-but-people-assume-he-is-adopted-because-people-in-wheelchairs-don't-have-sex son, and off to the checkout we went.I still to this day laugh at that!

The grocery store where I do the majority of my shopping at is the best! I am even going to mention their name... Buehlers. (And that is not a paid endorsement; that is my belief!) The employees of this store are always very helpful and would assist me in anyway with Max. After Max got over the shock that he was adopted... kidding!, he and I headed out to my van that day to head home.

Once Max climbed up into his chair seat, I would ask someone coming into the store or leaving if they would mind buckling my son's car seat. Never did I find that someone minded. I loved my independence with Max. Not that I did not worry about having him by myself. One of my biggest fears was if he should choke. I did not have the ability to help him! Therefore, Max never was allowed to eat, drink, or have small toys with him when I had him in the car by myself. I still to this day worry about it; however, he now knows and understands how to help himself, but I am still hyperaware. I will say it is a very helpless feeling. But I do not let myself get caught up in the feeling. I do plan things out more, but things happen.

I am proud to say my son is an active, relatively normal (he is thirteen, for gosh sakes) boy. Max and I are very close. I remember, when I was on bed rest at Akron General, I overhead a nurse say that it was very selfish of me to be having a baby. She went on to say that I could not even take care of myself, so how was I going to take care of a baby? I remember lying there thinking, *wow, this is coming from someone who works in the medical field.* I don't know why, but I think that people in the medical field, people who see trauma and suffering more often than most, would be more empathetic and understanding. Not always the case, as shown by this example.

I knew I was going to be a *great* mom. I could hold my child, feed my child, read to my child – many things that people without limitations do not do. But knowing that I could do these things did not stop me from getting caught up in wishing for the things I would want to do with my son. Go for a bike ride with him, walk through the woods with him, the little things that I saw people doing everyday with their children, not realizing how much of a gift that it was.

Then it came to me that I needed to stop wishing for those things and start doing the things I could do with my son.

Chapter Sixteen

One Day

It is 6:30 a.m. Most people wake to the sound of a beeping alarm or talk radio in the morning. I, on the other hand, wake to the joyous voice of the woman that has been getting my butt up every morning.

Monday thru Friday, for the last seven years, this woman has been coming into my house to assist me in getting up and starting my day. Her name is Joni, or Joan (which she hates). In addition to her real name, I have called her several different names throughout our years together. Let's see: I've called her 'Momma,' and there's really no reason why I call her that. And then there is 'Ju-Bear.' Again, I have no reason why I chose this nickname. But the good thing is that whatever I do call her, she answers to every name I've given her.

When Joni comes into the room, my morning routine starts. First things first, I need to use the bathroom. After that, Joni transfers me into my shower chair, which is made from PVC pipe with wheels. She helps me scrub up in the shower. Once we are done with the shower, we work on dressing my body from the waist up. Then it's back into bed to dress the rest of me.

From start to finish, the morning routine can take about an hour and a half. Of course, Don can help me get ready faster, but he has been doing it longer. Keep in mind though, when he gets me ready, I usually forgo putting on makeup, and if he had it his way, I would be sporting a ball cap! One of Don's famous sayings on the mornings that he has to get me ready is, "We need to cut corners, we are on a time frame!" I swear I am having that saying etched onto his tombstone when he goes!

Once I'm dressed and coiffed (big word!), my day really begins. The first thing I do is take care of our pups. We have two dogs that require a morning walk. The pups and I have a routine of taking a "poop walk" every morning. They seem to know that when I come into the kitchen all dressed, it's walk time. So off we will go on our morning walk.

The pup's names are Mr. Rocky Balboa and Mr. John Louis Montgomery, or Rocky and Lou for short. Rocky is a ten-pound Shih Tzu/Maltese mix and Lou is an eleven-pound, purebred Shih Tzu.

Before Rock and Lou came into our lives, I would always get the question, "Do you have an assistant dog?" I would respond, "No, but I am thinking of getting one." I periodically would do research on what would be the best breed to get, and it always came down to two kinds:

Labrador Retrievers and Golden Retrievers. And those are big dogs!

When Don and I were first married, we had a yellow lab named Ashley. We rescued her from a breeder who was mistreating her, and she turned out to be the sweetest dog ever! Of course, she was not trained in any way to help or assist me, but she did help out a lot when I dropped food on the floor.

Ashley was Max's first dog, too. She would let him crawl all over her when he was a baby, and she never minded him relentlessly wanting to sit on her. She was the best dog with him! As Max got older, our life style and schedules changed. Don and I realized we could not spend as much time with Ashley, so we gave her to a very loving family that had four active boys. It was a hard decision to make, but we knew she would get way more attention and exercise with this family. Luckily, we have many pictures of Max with Ashley, so he has those memories to hold forever.

Max was about nine when we got Rocky, and Lou came along a year after. Don swore he would never want little dogs, but these two dogs grew on him. They are the best! We do still get our big dog fix because our neighbors have a yellow lab named Rudy, so really we have the best of both worlds. We have big and little dog love but little dog poops!

After the morning walk with my pups, I head out to start my day. My days can be unpredictable depending on my son's schedule. Many are spent working around my son's schedule of basketball and fitness class or running him to a friend's house. A good friend of mine once said to me that for someone who supposedly has limited mobility, I am never home. And I must say that this is true. Between my speaking presentations, counseling job, and Max's schedule, I am hardly ever home. (I thank God for my mom, who helps me out with Max's schedule and serves as my backup.)

On this particular day, I have a speaking engagement in Kent. The program is a mandatory, court-ordered requirement for young adults between the ages of eighteen and twenty years old who have been arrested for underage drinking. I have been a speaker at this program for almost ten years and love participating in it. In this age group, I feel I can have a big impact on with my story.

The program includes four different presenters, including me. It is a two-hour program, and I am usually the anchor speaker. I usually leave my house early to get there before the program starts. For the longest time a good friend of mine drove me to the program because I was not comfortable driving that far. Over time and with practice, though, I became more comfortable driving farther distances, and now I love the time to myself in the car.

When I get there and all the participants are registered, the program gets started. The time goes by quickly for me, but I'm sure, for the people in the grey chairs, it's a bit burdensome to sit there for two hours. I am sure though that they are glad to be there rather than the alternative–jail. When it's over, some participants stay after to ask me questions, but usually they are eager to get out of there after all that sitting.

Then I head home. But before I start heading home, I call Max to check in and see what is going on. I do not have my phone accessible to me while I drive because I don't feel comfortable talking and driving. I do have my phone set to say who is calling me when I get incoming calls. That way, I know if it's important or not. If Max calls, I will pull over when I can and call him back.

I check in with Max and all is well, so now I start to head home. Of course, at this time of the day traffic is heavier, so it takes me longer to get home. The minute I come through my front door, I get a huge welcoming from my pups. And, like always, they expect a quick walk.

Once I'm back in the house, treats are distributed to the pups, and now I sit down with Max to see how his day was. Tonight, he has homework that we check over together. Sometimes though, Max waits for me to get home so we can go out and "shoot hoops" together. And yes, I shoot hoops. I guess you could say I am a "baller."

Shooting hoops with me is a bit of a challenge. It makes "street ball" a lot safer, injury-wise. I am usually required to guard Max and *try* to block his shots. That's all good, but I am about four feet tall sitting, of course, and Max is almost six feet. When we play, I sit out there waving my one arm as high as I can to try to "get in his face." With my other hand, I am driving my chair, bobbing and weaving the best I can. I do all this and try not to ram him in the shins, snap his ankle, and end any future of a basketball career. This is not an easy task for me!

But I do it because I love being outside with him and actually doing something that he loves to do! We play this jump-out-of-mom's-way-so-she-doesn't-injure-me game for maybe a half hour or so before Don gets home from work. Once Don gets home, he and I will have coffee and talk about our days. Tonight, Don is in charge of making dinner, so while he is doing that, Max and I continue to go over any homework he's having trouble with, and I check my emails.

Once dinner is over, the evening will go one of two ways. It can be a quiet evening at home watching T.V. or it can involve more running around, taking Max to a practice or going to the store for something. This night happens to be a basketball practice night. After dinner, Max gathers all his gear together and off he and I go. I take him to practices so Don can stay home and clean up after dinner and do stuff around the house.

Max's practice tonight is about an hour away. To keep myself occupied, I take stuff to do while he is playing. Usually, I take schoolwork to read or a magazine, but most of the time I end up talking with the other parents the whole time, which is fine, too.

On the way home, Max will be starving, so we stop at a nearby McDonald's. He and I will go through the drive-thru, which will bring all kinds of stares when I pull up to pay. The look on the workers faces is priceless. They usually try not to act surprised, which always makes me laugh because there are not a lot of drivers out there with the driving equipment I have. They usually are taken aback a bit to see all the equipment and hand controls in my souped-up van. Some will muster up enough bravery to say how cool all of it is. Others will just have a look of amazement on their faces and wait until I pull away to say something to a co-worker. I know this because I watch them in my rearview mirror.

When I have someone with me, they can hand the money to the worker and take the food when they hand it out. When I go to a drive-thru alone (which I just started doing five years ago), I can hand the worker the money (which is usually my bank card, because then I do not have to worry about handling money), but I then ask the window person if I can pull forward and have someone bring my food out. I have the person set the food on my front passenger seat and off I go. I don't eat in my car when I am by myself because it is too hard to manage the food on my own. Once I get the food, I head home, where Max or Don will come out and get the stuff off the seat.

Having stopped at McDonalds after Max's practice, I do not get anything to eat. I will maybe get a drink, but usually I end up finishing Max's drink. If I am driving, the person sitting next to me is in charge of holding my drink while I drive, and what ends up happening is I just say, "drink please," which is my co-pilots cue to hold my drink in front of me. So, if you're my co-pilot, you are working!

On our rides home from long distance practices, I love the 'talk-time' that I get with Max. There is no radio on; it's just me and him talking. We have our fun 'question games' that we play, like "what is your favorite movie" or "who is your favorite actor?" Or we will say a line from one of our favorite movies, and the other person has to guess the movie. I treasure these rides and memories because I know that not too far in the future, he will be driving himself to practices and our talk-times will be no more.

Once we are home Max hits the shower, and I spend some time with Don. It is usually close to ten o'clock when we get home, so the 'Don time' is not real long because after all that running around, I am ready for bed.

I wash my face and brush my teeth then Don helps me get undressed and into my pjs. Then he transfers me into bed. I will say too, this is the best feeling–getting into bed at night–because I can stretch out and lay flat. Remember,

I have been in the sitting position since about seven-thirty in the morning. Yes, I have been transferred out of my chair for bathroom breaks, but for the most part, I have been sitting *all day*!

Don and I spend some more quality time watching TV in bed. But shortly after I get into bed, I am out like a light! Don always says that once I ask to be rolled onto my side, I seem to fall asleep instantly. I will of course deny that this occurs, but within minutes of turning, I drift off to dreamland.

It's a rare occasion that I sleep through the night. I usually wake Don up once or twice to help me reposition or roll to my other side. When people would say to Don and I that they bet we were happy once Max started sleeping through the night, we would say, "Oh, yes," and look at each other. Once we were out of ear shot, Don would say, "Now if I could just get my wife to." This was our funny inside joke we would say to each other. Let's be real: most people can't understand the lifestyle of someone with a physical disability like mine, let alone the life of a person married to someone with my disability.

My family has a way of life that only another family living with someone who has a similar disability can understand. We have really good friends, a husband and wife, where the husband is a quadriplegic. They have been married a little longer then we have, and they have twin daughters that are almost, to the day, one year older than

Max. The nice thing about getting together with them, besides seeing each other (which is great!), is that Pam, the wife, gives me her perspective as the spouse married to someone in a wheelchair. I then can give Pam my perspective. It's really a neat thing, talking as women about our lives and the challenges and joys they bring. Our children also have a unique bond, having one of their parents in a wheelchair.

At night, when my day is over and I am on my side about to fall asleep, I say my prayers and thank God for the day that I got to enjoy and the things that I can do. I have been blessed with this incredible child. I can breathe on my own, move my arms, and drive myself around. Many people may look at me and how I now live my life and say there is no way I could do that. But no one ever knows what strength they have within themselves to live until they chose to start living their life. Once I stopped wishing that this crash never happened to me and started living my life, I was able to see the blessings I still had. And for those, which I find in great abundance, I thank God every day!

Chapter Seventeen

Lessons Learned

I live in Ohio with Don and Max. We have the same blessings and challenges that every other family does. I write (this book, for example) and speak to various groups for a living. Sometimes I do standup comedy. As for the future, I may be disabled, but I'm not clairvoyant; I have no more of an idea about what's around the bend than you do. You now know way more about my life than I'll ever know about yours, but please don't define me by my disability. Sure, it's part of my life, but it's not the most important part. I hope that what you've learned in the last couple of hundred pages is that my name is Barb, I'm from Ohio, I have a husband named Don and a son named Max, and I've had some interesting things happen to me. Have I learned some lessons along the way? Absolutely. Let me share some of them with you.

This is the only life we get, so stop wishing for another one.

We are all in the middle of the only life we will ever get. There is no *other* life that we could live instead of this one. While there *could* be an alternate universe where I am not in a wheelchair and the Statue of Liberty is a man wearing pants painted bright red, this isn't it, and I have no idea where the door to it might be found. We have to work at making this life work out.

Have I ever wished I wasn't in this chair? Of course. But I also wish I was taller, looked like a Victoria's Secret model, could sing with perfect pitch, had an uncanny ability to learn foreign languages, and would be discovered to be the long-lost heir to the British throne. Those are fantasies, and it's fun to toss them around in my head, like dreaming I could fly. But once you start wishing one thing about your life was different, where does that stop? Self-pity is a slippery slope that I've never wanted to start down. If I had a different life, I wouldn't have Don and Max in it. I wouldn't have seen what I've seen, learned what I've learned, or become who I am. I wouldn't be *me* to be here wishing I *wasn't* me (wrap your brain around that paradox!). In other words, it's all just speculation and imagination. And every minute I waste daydreaming I wish I wasn't me is another minute that I don't have to spend making my actual life as good as it can possibly be.

Control what you can and react well to what you can't.

I should have not gotten in that car that night. Given the circumstances, it wasn't the smart choice. Sure, we might have gotten away with it—just taken a ride and ended up back at the party. In fact, the odds were in our favor that it would have been nothing more than a joyride by a couple of buzzed teenagers. But why tempt fate? Why take risks we don't need to take? There are a thousand accidents waiting to shipwreck our lives every day. Why make it easier for misfortune to strike?

Whenever and wherever we do have control, we should use it wisely.

But even if I had been smart enough to not get into that car, or not drink at that party in the first place, something else could have put me in this chair. A drunk driver could have run a red light and T-boned me on my way to church on a Sunday morning. We can't control all the circumstances of life. We could seal ourselves up in a bunker with food and weapons like we were waiting for the zombies to come and a can of beans could fall off the shelf and crack our skull. It's risky to be alive.

So life is finding the balance between controlling what you can and coping with what you can't. There are no guarantees for how life will turn out. But we can control our character—even a spine injury cannot rob us of goodness, the ability to treat people the right way, and the courage to work hard and grow a little bit every day. No injury can make you a bitter, angry jerk. Only you can do that.

It doesn't take long for your life to change, but it doesn't *have to* change.

Before the accident, I was an outgoing, busy, largely happy person. I had parents that loved me but yelled at me when I did something wrong. I enjoyed a joke, I couldn't stand to sit still for too long, and I wanted to meet people and have as much fun with them as I could. Then, in the blink of an eye, I lost the ability to walk ever again.

But I didn't stop being me. I was just me in a chair. I still had a family that loved each other and argued, I still liked to hear or crack a joke and laugh out loud, and I still wanted to meet people and have as much fun with them as I could. I still couldn't stand to sit still, and that obviously presented a problem for someone in a wheelchair. So I had to tweak my preferences: now I can't stand for my chair to be still for too long. I'm still the same person; I just look at the world from a foot lower than I used to.

Circumstances and physical abilities are impermanent. Jobs come and go. Houses burn down and get washed away in floods. Arms and legs and organs can all stop working well. But your identity, your personality, your perspective on life? Cheerful kids become cheerful grownups and eventually cheerful old people telling jokes in the nursing home. Grumpy, gloomy, griping kids are often a pain in everyone's rear ends forever, regardless of how much is in their bank account or how low their cholesterol is. Focus on character and personality. If you're not the person you'd like to be, work hard at changing.

If It's Funny, Laugh At It.

I'm convinced that God has a sense of humor.

Life isn't always fun, but there's almost always something funny around you if you keep your eyes open. A lot of things in life demand serious attention, and some of them are deadly serious. But we have to be careful not to take everything too seriously, especially ourselves. I think that's a gift: God sometimes plays practical jokes on us by giving us crappy days that turn out to be like those little plastic piles of fake dog poop. Sometimes, what looks terrible is only mildly irritating and would be potentially hilarious if it happened to someone else.

You know it's an old cliché that "laughter is the best medicine." But the reason that clichés become clichés is that they're often true. There are no cures (yet) for my spinal injuries. But I can laugh at myself and admit the absurdity of some of the situations I find myself in. That's been a pretty powerful way to cope with the challenges in my life. It's cheaper and healthier than drugs or psychoanalysis. In fact, psychologists have provided some of the funnier episodes in my story. They are the source of some of my best material.

So don't grip the wheel of life so tight that you can't giggle regularly and even full-out guffaw on occasion. It's better to go through life with a twinkle in your eye than a glare. For goodness sake, you only live once. Lighten up.

There Are No Excuses For Not Loving Someone.

After my last point, let me be at least a little bit serious (just for a moment). I could have let my disappointment fester into bitterness and rot my soul from the inside out. I didn't for the reasons above. But I also could have become so embarrassed by my body, so self-conscious of my condition, that I never opened myself up to an intimate relationship. I could have built an emotional wall and put practical distance between anyone other than the professionals who got paid to care for me. Heck, there are people who are able-bodied who do that.

But why would we want to go through life without love? Oh sure, someone could say, no one will ever be able to love me with all my deficiencies and baggage. Maybe, maybe not. But one thing is certain: if you hide behind that wall, retreat to the far side of no-man's land, no one ever will be able to.

But it's not just enough to make yourself available for love and then wait for it to come to you. That's a low-percentage shot. Stack the odds of finding love by *initiating* it. Love someone else. I'm going to go out on a limb here and suggest that it almost doesn't matter who you start loving. Love your neighbor, your caregiver, a family member, the kid you tutor, the bus driver, your prison guard, whoever. The act of feeling and giving love changes you. It has inherent value, it's worth it for its own sake, even if it never gets returned.

I know that someone out there is saying, but what if I put myself out there, initiate love, and get rejected? Sure, that can be excruciatingly painful. But there are different kinds of pain. There's the pain of a broken leg or a broken heart. It hurts like hell—for a while. But if you learn all the lessons I did, you realize that you can overcome that kind of hurt. A deeper, more corrosive pain comes from letting your heart atrophy and your soul wither. To go through life shut up in some lonely prison of your own mind? That is a pain that will last for eternity.

Everything Adds Up, For Better Or Worse.

There are big, dramatic moments in life when we are aware that we are facing a decision that will affect us forever: agreeing to get married and stuff like that.

But every day we make lots of little decisions, and those have a way of adding up. If you spend money like a sailor on shore leave, your odds of future financial security drop dramatically. If you party and drink and drive home often enough, the odds of something bad happening keep going up. Sure, you might get away with it, but nothing is completely free of consequences.

It goes the other way, too. Love, laughter, loyalty—all of these things play out over time. You become known as a likable and reliable person to have around. The odds of you being surrounded by good people who will stick with you through bad times start stacking up in your favor.

As our cumulative choices stack up over time, they begin to tilt our fate one way or the other. As a teenager, my drinking and partying led to that car ride and my ride in this chair. But it's just as true that the way my family taught me to see the world made it more likely that I would be resilient and be able to roll with and even overcome the challenges of life.

So pay careful attention to your little choices. They are always pointing you down one road or another.

We Are Not Alone.

What we do affects others, and what they do affects us. This is good news because it means that we can positively affect the world. Most of us are not rich or powerful (if you're reading this and you *are* rich and powerful, please consider buying 100,000 copies of this book and appointing me ambassador to Tahiti). Left to ourselves, our leverage to change the world is pretty limited.

But if we can influence others, our reach gets a lot longer. You know how these exponential change examples go: if one person influences two other people, and each of them influences two more, and so on, eventually you affect the planet. Well, that might be a little bit ambitious, but the point is the same. Because we are not alone we have more power for positive change than we ever imagined. The trick is to build your networks and be a positive enough person that you earn the right and respect to be heard. You can make the world a better place.

But this is also bad news because your negativity can spread just as easily. You don't want to be a spreader of nasty ideas and crappy attitudes. We've got an epidemic of that, so keep it to yourself. I may not be rich, literally or figuratively, but in all my speaking and writing, I want to be spreading pennies, not stealing and hoarding them. Make the world a better place by doing some good for someone today. Pay it forward and all that.

Start Living Your Actual Life.

Start living your real life right now because the alternative is... what, exactly? This is the only life any of us will get, and the clock is ticking.

When you listen to doctors and nurses and chaplains—professionals who spend a lot of time with the dying—they say that almost everyone on their deathbed wishes for two things. First, that they *had* spent more time with their family, loving the people closest to them. Second, they wish that they had *more* time—more time to spend with their family and doing something significant with their life.

So, unless we are completely stupid (and I don't think our stupidity is *complete*), we'd be wise to listen to their regrets and plan our route through life to avoid the same mistakes. Don't screw around and waste another hour wishing you were someone else. You're not, so knock it off. You're you, and if you want to get anywhere in life, that journey starts right now from where you're sitting while you read this. Get busy.

You Do Not Have To Know How To Spell *"Czechoslovakia!"*

I remember when Patrick the Psychologist asked me to spell *Czechoslovakia* to prove that I didn't have a brain injury. It was an idiotic test because I couldn't spell it before the accident. It proved nothing. In fact, if I could have spelled *Czechoslovakia* it would have been proof that the accident had given me superpowers ("Spelling Girl!").

Here's my point, and I'll end the book with this: life is not about trick questions. The really important stuff is pretty straightforward. Love God and your neighbor as yourself. Don't spend more than you make or drink before you drive. Get a good night's sleep, show up to work on time every day, and finish stuff you started. Wipe that smirk off your face and drop the bad attitude. Leave places cleaner than you found them and the world a better place than when you got here. Love someone and laugh about something before you go to bed tonight.

About the Author

At the age of eighteen, Barb's decision to get into a car with a high school friend after they both had been drinking alcohol is one she will live with for the rest of her life.

Today, her story may change the rest of yours.

As a speaker, comedian, and author, Barb is using her personal story and life-lessons to help change the way people perceive and live their own lives. Barb believes everyone faces a life challenge at some point. She stresses the importance of believing in one's self, and building as well as maintaining, a support system. She also focuses on the crucial role humor and attitude can play in the decisions we make and how we overcome challenges.

Made in the USA
Lexington, KY
24 January 2013